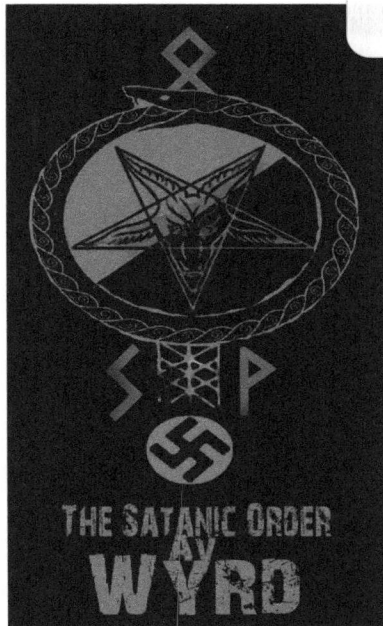

THE SATANIC ORDER
AV
WYRD

The Satanic Order av Wyrd

The Concise Collection

Imp K. Lokessen

The Satanic Order av Wyrd

Nephilim Press © 2023

ISBN: 978-1-957758-17-6

To Robert C. W., Mathilde Fae, Angela Victoria, Avalee Elizabeth, David Walker, Daniel P., Joseph W., Jean L., Mick G. H., Randy B., Stefan R., Andy S., the Punks, the Metal-Heads, Those Who Seek Truth, Those who Challenge Authority, Anarcho-Communists, All Satanic Organizations, All Fraternal Orders and Individuals Using Black Magick, the Readers of This Book, and Our Beloved Satan, Loke!

Thank you for your time.

Contents

Introduction Part I: It's Self-Deceit, and It Just Won't Do!. 1

Introduction Part II: Why Are You Starting at the End? 7

Introduction Part III: On Chaos 9

Introduction Part IV: On Cosmic Energy. 11

I   An Origin Story, Its Fate, and Loke 15

     On Reverent Amalgam 20
     The Satan, Loke 21
     The Satan, Loke, Represents. 23
     Symbols of the Satan, Loke. 24
     Why Loke?. 25
     The Answer to the Question (and I Hope This Isn't Too Crass) "Why
       Loke?": 27
     Loke's Role in the Satanic Order av Wyrd 28
     For Your Consideration or Those to Be Admitted 29

II   Our Views and Their Practical Applications—Section I 31

     The Concept of Yggdrasil and the Nine (10) Realms 31
     The Nine (10) Realms 31
     Seithr and Galdr/Wyrd and Orlog Command:
       Applied to Cosmic Energy 33
     What You'll Need. 34
     Aligning with Yggdrasil 34
     More Tools for Ritual Purposes. 38

The SOW Method-Astral Projection. 40

III Our Views and Their Practical Applications—Section II—
Cosmic Energy: Science and Theory. 45

Cosmic Energy Frequencies. 46
Social Darwinism and Racial Hygiene. 48
How to Protect and Empower Your Cosmic Energy Field 49
Lokean Armor 52
Labradorite 54
The Natural Quartz. 55
Loke's Snare. 55

IV Our Views and Their Practical Applications—Section III—Fear 57

Example I—The Terroristic Toxic Gas Incident—1995 58
Example II—The Tennessee High School Toxic Gas Incident of 1998 58
Example III—Strawberries with Sugar Virus of 2006 59
Operant Conditioning. 66
The VI Phases of Pain 67
        Phase I—The Humiliation Declaration 68
        Phase II—The Revealing of Truths 69
        Phase III—The Pilfering Pick-Me-Up. 70
        Phase IV—The Scales of Skirmish. 71
        Phase V—The Death Directive. 73
        Phase VI—The Rest Stop Repeat 75

V The Shadow Self and the Realization of the Alterna Unu 77

The Shadow Self 77
The Alterna Unu. 79
Step I: Locating Your Alterna Unu 82
Step II: Capturing Your Alterna Unu 83
The II Phases of the Alterna Unu Alliance. 84
        Phase I—Identify and Ally 84
        Phase II—Capturing Your Alterna Unu. 85

VI Political Views within the Satanic Order av Wyrd 87

Why Politics? 88
The Three Versions of Politics 89
Liberalism, Conservatism, and Capitalism 89
Syncretism. 92
Anarchy. 93
Stateless Communism. 94

VII Additional Rituals and Their Objectives 97

The Black Mass..98
Participants..99
Prepping the Temple 99
The Ceremony...99
The Death Ritual 104
  Participants (all will wear black robes) 105
  The Ceremony 105
  The Satanic Blessing...................................107
Sigils and Talismans 108
The Primary, Applicable Association to the Satanic Order av Wyrd 108
The Lesser Key of Solomon.................................109
Chaos Magick 130
Atavistic Nostalgia.......................................131
Germanic and Norse Sigils or Staves 135
The Valknut...138
The Confidential Order av Wyrd............................141

VIII The Vaesen and the Fae 143

The Vaesen 144
The Fae...151

IX Additional Figures Honored by SOW: The Figures av Glory ...159

X   The Satanic Order av Wyrd—Imperative and Requisite Reading 9

Narratives and Nonfiction 170
Norse Theology, Cosmology, and Folklore 171
Black Magick..171
Anarcho-Communism 172

It's Self-Deceit, and It Just Won't Do!

T his piece, philosophy, and ideology/methodology is not meant to discourage or offend, anyone. In the great words of Thomas Paine, "I put the following work under your protection. It contains my opinions upon religion. You will do me the justice to remember that I have always strenuously supported the right of every man to his own opinion, however different that opinion might be to mine. He who denies another this right, makes a slave of himself to his present opinion, because he precludes himself the right of changing it."

That being said, there are those who deliberately choose to deny or reject outside opinion on the grounds that it may directly clash with their own personal beliefs. In this sense, it would be an offense to their deeply held beliefs and a complete waste of time to hear that of the opposition. Furthermore, there are those who were previously made aware of whatever the opposition had to offer and, therefore, would have yet another reason to reject the opposition. In other words, "he who denies another this right" frees himself from becoming fuel for someone else's fire and, if he's willing to take the chance of possibly wasting precious time or fanning someone else's flames in order to better suit that person's pride and his/her, most likely, unwarranted self-inflated image, sobeit. As for me, I have better ways to spend my fucking time.

My way of thinking is not akin to the aforementioned, and I dare say I'm quite an admirer of Thomas Paine's. If you are someone, however, who thinks more or less in this particularly crass, ignorant, stubborn fashion or agrees with this way of being entirely, then you may want to reconsider. This method is fraught with arrogance and is a path that will only lead to an overwhelming number of forks and just as many dead ends. Unfortunately, sooner or later, the only direction left to go is back from which you came.

We've all been there once or twice in our lives, and that's okay. We've all made mistakes. We've all been victims of or created hypocrisy in our lives or in the lives of others. We've all been led astray or led others astray and possibly as a result of previously being led astray.

Unfortunately, there are too many of us who don't learn from our mistakes and repeat those mistakes, expecting different results. This is uncalled for. This is a minuscule but very dumbfounding form of madness, and it just won't do. We must avoid repetition of mistakes and hypocrisy. Forget the condition or selective act of denying yourself progressive, positive change and general knowledge. Otherwise, you're only lying to yourself, pulling the wool over your very own eyes, hoodwinked at your discretion. Is this what you want? Is this how you'd be remembered?

But it's a learning process, a path fraught with stepping stones that lead to bigger and better things. If you manage to reach your destination, supreme greatness and unimaginable power will be yours.

It was William Shakespeare who wrote, "To thine own self be true!" Those words that were written so long ago are so powerful that they still resonate with billions of people on the planet and for good reason: It's one of the truest statements known to mankind.

Stated simply, the ensuing content may provide support into an ideology in which one may have never considered before or, perhaps, many have considered and were reluctant to pursue; and I hope that you extract enjoyment, wisdom, and/or insight from the following text:.

In light of self-deceit, a considerably tangential approach, but the necessary path, nonetheless: Consider the not at all subjective case that religion, as a whole, that is to say, a particular set of beliefs that is organized and has become indoctrinated and/or popularized by the masses, unfortunately reaches a state of derivation, filtered and extracted, through one book or another, virtually diminishing its own purpose or message or goal. Eventually, as a result of this filtration system, and because of the trail in the system's wake, the result in any rational realm of perception is hypocrisy, inconsistency, and relentless, counterproductive internal and external dilemmas that erode from the inside out and vice versa.

Christianity or what Christianity has become is the forerunner and beacon of this process, and I feel, simultaneously, sympathy and hatred for these Christians who are blinded and coaxed or herded into this form of consciousness. It's dangerous, alienating, ignorant behavior, and it just won't do! The following are excerpts and facts that give testament to this system of hypocrisy, as well as misinterpretation, and its aftermath.

1. Christ isn't Jesus's surname. Christ is a title, derived from the Greek verb meaning "anointed one."

2. Satan isn't Satan's name. Satan is a position or title meaning "the accuser" or "the adversary" and there are ancient Hebrew scriptures that predate the Bible that state in specific detail that there have been multiple fallen angels and rulers of hell, some of whom still serve God.

3. Jesus's birthday wasn't on Christmas, and he wasn't resurrected on Easter. In fact, many of the dates that promote the so-called Christian holidays take place on these dates for two reasons:

   a. The first reason is that the Bible is an astrological-theological hybrid and carries with it dates corresponding directly with the zodiac and the sun, and that's how it's always been.

   b. The second reason is that everyone who was celebrating the zodiac and the sun and the solstices and the so-called old or obsolete gods were pagan or heathen, and the Christians did not like that one bit. Fortunately, those celebrations and the practices therein were too difficult for Christians to overcome, and they also risked persecution by the inhabitants for their own newfound beliefs. So the Christians created their ecclesiastical calendar around the heathen celebrations and practices to cover up and/**or** eventually eliminate them. Obviously, that move wasn't completely successful, for we still practice pagan and/or heathen traditions on those so-called Christian holidays.

4. Christian holidays and their heathen counterparts are as follows: Christmas caroling is derived from an act called *wassailing*, during which people would sing in groups to the wealthy or wealthier or the gods for gifts or for good harvest in their fields, orchards, and vineyards. Wreaths were originally gifts during Roman festivities, something Christians adopted to save themselves from persecution. Mistletoe was a druid, Norse, and Native American tool for peace and joy and to protect against lightning and other negative effects of bad weather. Santa Claus is derived from the Norse god, Odin. The Yule log is a pagan tradition as well. Easter is derived from Eostre, a pagan goddess celebrated around the spring solstice. The Easter bunny is derived from Eostre as a symbol of fertility and the German Osterhase: a bunny that brought eggs to good children. Eggs and the decorating of eggs in easter are also symbols of new life and rebirth in pagan practices. There are other holidays that we celebrate that are not Christian, but based on pagan practices and beliefs.

5. The comparative messages between the Old and New Testaments of the Christian Bible are rife with hypocrisy and misinterpretation: A man can divorce his wife for any reason, and both can remarry (Deuteronomy 24:1, 2). Divorce is wrong, and remarriage is adultery (Mark 10:11, 12). Adam sinned. Therefore, all men are condemned to death (Romans 5:12, 19; 1 Corinthians 15:22). Children are not to suffer for their parent's sins (Deuteronomy 24:16; 2 Kings14:6; 2 Chronicles 25:4; Ezekiel 18:20). God is vengeful Genesis 4:15; Deuteronomy 32:35; Ezekiel 25:14–17; Nahum 1:2; Romans 12:19; Hebrews 10:30). God is a warrior (Exodus 15:3; Isaiah 42:13; Psalm 24:8). God is a consuming fire (Deuteronomy 4:24; Deuteronomy 9:3; Hebrews 12:29). God is jealous (Exodus 20:5; Exodus 34:14; Deuteronomy 4:24; Deuteronomy

5:9; Deuteronomy 6:15; Deuteronomy 29:20; Deuteronomy 32:21). God murders and kills (Numbers 31:7, 17; Deuteronomy 20:16, 17; Joshua 10:40; Judges 14:19; Ezekiel 9:5, 6; Numbers 11:33). God is angry (Numbers 32:14; Numbers 25:3, 4; Deuteronomy 6:15; Deuteronomy 9:7, 8; Deuteronomy 29:20; Deuteronomy 32:21; Psalm 7:11; Psalm 78:49; Jeremiah 4:8; Jeremiah 17:4; Jeremiah 32:30, 31; Zephaniah 2:2; 2 Samuel 22:8, 9; Ezekiel 6:12). God is love and peace (2 Corinthians 13:11, 14; 1 John 4:8,16; Romans 15:33). God's spirit inspires love, peace, and so on (Galatians 5:22, 23). God never changes (Malachi 3:6). The lord is good to all and his tender mercies are over all his works (Psalm 145:9). And I will dash them, one against the other, even the fathers and the sons together, saith the lord: I will not pity, nor spare, nor have mercy, but destroy them (Jeremiah 13:14).

I'll stop here. I'm sure you've had enough. But you need to be made aware that there are over sixty contradictions between the Old and New Testaments, nearly two hundred contradictions within the New Testament alone, and over one hundred contradictions within the Old Testament alone.

As for the aftermath, societies of the world turned on each other, as well as the Earth. The beautiful and nurturing ways of the old world, predominantly, but not limited to, the days before Christ, were replaced by a judging and dictating sky god, and often enough, the transition was harshly imposed by those who would gain power by their new views. New concepts swept across Europe with warriors on newly domesticated horses. The concept of warfare walled cities across the world. Subjugation and personal wealth took over. Even in areas where the transition was less forceful, it was accompanied by a lessening of all life, experiences we saw horribly mirrored in the treatment of Native Americans, Africans, Chinese, Irish, Scottish, and so on.

Each of these deities and their priests, monks, pastors, ministers, whatever you want to call them, have struggled to find wisdom in their own lies, even if their beliefs, by chance, didn't derive from a lie. They've tried to force others to do the same, and 2.2 billion people fucking bought it! But this can only last so long before more beliefs are created and abolish the past, while taking on identical forms, for we all know that the past reflects the future and vice versa.

Why Are You Starting at the End?

D o not mistake the things I've said thus far. They may seem to denounce a wide range of subject matter deemed important by man. On the contrary, I've only discouraged those who lack a complete knowledge of what they believe and choose to believe their belief with complete devotion as well as those who use fragmented bases to get and give their answers, as a result of their lacking complete knowledge.

Let it be known: the first introduction barely scratches the surface, nor does it give justice to the underbelly. That was a glimpse into the plague that is self-deceit and hypocrisy. I'm not saying that these gods and goddesses are not out there. In a sense, I encourage you to believe that they are out there. What I'm proposing and asking of you is to come to the realization that you may never know the absolute truth of our existence and the afterlife, and if you must pursue truth—and I hope you do—go to the source or foundation and embrace your belief, if you manage to establish a belief,

for what it really is. Yes, certain transformations are necessary to solidify the belief where it was rather inconclusive before. But you be the judge of that and the level of its necessity. Don't start at the end. Why are you starting at the end? If you start there, there's no opportunity to move forward or progress, and if you do move forward or progress, you'll have to turn back, eventually, because your foundation will be shaky with no substantial origin or history.

There are so many philosophies of the world, but only a very small sum can stick to their beliefs. Most would treat their beliefs as guidelines rather than abide by every little concept of which that particular belief consists, resulting, once more, in an act of perpetual self-deceit. Even those who stick to their beliefs and are certain that their beliefs have foundations and factual existence will undergo paradigms and paradoxes; and as paradigms change, so does the absolute truth, and as paradoxes occur, so does absolute confusion. Therein lies yet another dilemma (for most): that paradigm and paradoxical shifts occur and that the absolute truth is changing consistently. In addition, many perceive true paradigm and paradoxical shifts to take place, on a higher plane, every few thousand years, to some, every few hundred years, to others, even less. In truth, paradigm and paradoxical shifts take place consistently within many divisions of religion, philosophy, mathematics, and science on a regular basis, in a plethora of ways, in matters of months, days, even minutes, and pinpointing those shifts is futile. As a result, the time that many afford themselves to accomplish their goals and the time on which many base their foundations and biases toward these goals is undoubtedly skewed and altered, becoming a sort of unforeseeable obstacle and an endless battle.

There are only two truths that remain constant in this realm otherwise laden with hypocrisy and paradigm changes and paradoxical shifts. One of those is Chaos; the other is Cosmic Energy, or Wyrd. These always flowing, always changing manifestations never change! Maniacal ravings of a madman? Perhaps.

On Chaos

Y ou are; therefore, you suffer Chaos. Chaos has touched all places in every chronological aspect and the lives of every mature individual. Chaos is cosmic. In everyone, somewhere within, are feelings unjustifiably developed, the torturer, the sadist, the ravisher, the killer, as well as feelings of the otherwise opposite nature. To some small extent, you allow the more negative feelings to entertain, but you nearly always perceive that cause as coming from the outside, an external occurrence, an antagonism from another source that affected and effected a certain personal state of things, never admitting that it most likely emanates from within yourself, everyone, every creature, every place, everything, full of mystery, an animalistic urge from the very beginnings of life, an action that exceeds explanation and boundaries, Chaos! Chaos is alive in the sufferings and the pleasures of the world, and when these instances of Chaos have elapsed, there will be others,

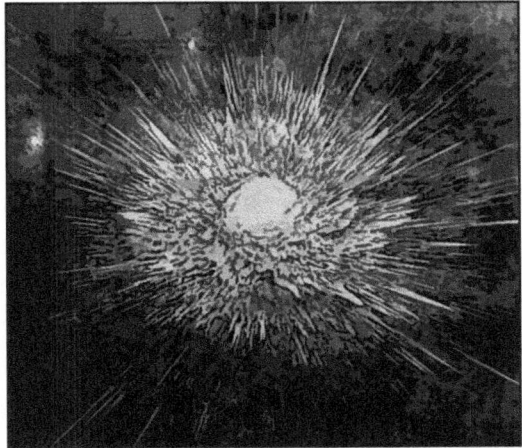

each an infliction of torment and ecstasy, absolute, demanding our atten-tion. Chaos belongs to no religion, no one being, nothing, but Chaos embraces all, a timeless condition, not a social circumstance. Chaos is the universe and the multiverse, the first and foremost truth.

Some may say that order will spring from Chaos and all will be revealed, leaving the inhabitants of the world fully evolved and in an omniscient state and possibly transcended and liberated from this planet into the afterlife: the big-picture argument. But who could possibly claim that they know the big picture and who poses the idea of this big picture in the first place? God? Another philosopher? A supercomputer? The end result of human existence and our evolutionary state will most likely be a result of human action, and a negative one at that; and this creator in question, predominantly the Christian god, is, as stated by the concept's creator, a being of pure freedom, which is the reason we were supposedly given freedom, and is, therefore, free to be evil or righteous on a regular basis, as clearly conveyed by the Old and New Testaments. This is a being of pure chaos. He/she/it, this god, may not be con-cerned with the affairs of Earth at all. This, if nothing else, should be known by Christian believers, because, under the wide range of their concept's moral and religious goodness, are pride, hate, and hypocrisy, complete confusion, in other words, chaos. Unfortunately, these very same followers won't accept the base concept of Chaos, because they are self-contradictory animals, and their creative and destructive powers come from much of the same source.

One of my many minor beliefs is that it would be better to reign in hell than have to spend a lifetime and countless amounts of money figuring out what is right and what is wrong. Monstrous acts aren't always created by monsters. Torturers often make successful husbands and devoted fathers. Those who steal pension funds and pollute regions of the planet are usually mild-mannered indi-viduals. But these chaotic occurrences are here and creating a reason for these occurrences is asinine, because it's Chaos. It's nature and the universe, and it is what it is. It is a fact that most of the concepts regarding goodness are results of particular man-made systems, but those who serve these systems may very well be unaware of the gravity of their own actions and, often enough, cause much more disorder through the segregation of everything they're for and against. It's unrealistic for their cause, and it's, once again, self-deceit.

On Cosmic Energy

The second undeniable truth is Cosmic Energy, or Chi, or bioenergy, or electromagnetic energy, and so on, that we are all intimately and, often, unknowingly, but, intrinsically, sometimes through an extreme intuition, connected, somehow, to Earth and the universe or multiverse, whether we're aware or not and whether we question it or not. It's just a strange physical, sometimes emotional, feeling. In a time when many religions and other belief systems separate us from gods and goddesses, place us above animals, separate us from each other, and kill us off, (1) the realization and coexistence with chaos, (2) knowing the underlying concept of being connected to Earth and the multiverse, (3) and the pursuit of truth, personal and otherwise, via roots or essence or the heart or foundation will lead to self-gratification and a higher form of being and, as previously mentioned, supreme greatness and unimaginable power will be yours.

Various cultures throughout history up to our present era have had their own ways of honing in on cosmic energy or exercising their own cosmic energy for many reasons, such as achievement of enlightenment, connection with supreme consciousness or intelligence, complete self-awareness, maintenance of universal balance, nourishment of body cells and the support of internal organs and their functions, and promotion of happiness and general well-being, and so on. In addition to these or on a separate path completely, scientists have also pursued cosmic or electromagnetic energy as early as the eighteenth century. The overall hypothesis or theory behind it is nearly identical to that of those who have a more reverent or spiritual approach.

The following is a timeline of accounts concerning cosmic energy in the western and eastern world:

- 40,000 BC: Yoga, originating in Egypt, but commonly associated with Hinduism, coined the concept of Prana, meaning "life-force." Pranayama, meditation, mantras, and the like are all practices that embrace the concept of Prana and serve as implementations to achieve nearly all the objectives addressed in the previous paragraph.

- Roughly 1200 BC–CE fifteenth century: Starting with Germanic Paganism and transitioning into Norse Theology, Orlog is the individual's Wyrd, Wyrd being primarily, but not limited to, fate. The Wyrd is essentially a boundless web of energy with countless layers that connect everyone and everything. Through practices such as Seithr and Galdr, one could strengthen their energy or spirit or Orlog for a multitude of reasons analogous to the objectives addressed previously as well as to manipulate aspects of the physical Earth realm and to travel to other realms within the universe, kindred to astral projection.

- Roughly 1120s BC–early 200s BC: Within the years of the pre-Han dynasty, already aware of qi/chi/ki (universal/spiritual energy), China developed breathing techniques and acupuncture reflex techniques as well as physical dances and exercises to remove energetic disturbances, obtain health, and improve overall vital longevity. Mainly practiced by Daoist and Confucian scholars, these techniques were only used for health or medical purposes.

- Prehistory–CE 320s: Hawaiian cultures practice Huna to manipulate a life-force energy, Mana.

- Eighteenth century: Franz Anton Mesmer, a German physicist and astronomy enthusiast, gained international popularity by posing the idea that the universe is one living unity and, to maintain health, one needed to maintain balance of forces of the living universe.

Mesmer believed that this force could be transferred from one being to another through Animal Magnetism.

- 1840s: Baron Carl von Reichenbach, a German chemist, geologist, metallurgist, and so on, as the result of all of his research, maintains that the force that underlies all natural forces is something called the Odic Force, named after the Norse god, Odin.
- 1860s–1920s: Mikao Usui, a Japanese Buddhist doctor, studied in the west and in China. In China, however, he meditated and fasted for twenty-one days on Mount Kurama, where he allegedly gained heightened awareness and discovered Reiki (God Energy). He opened his first clinic in Tokyo.
- 1880s–1940s: Ethereal Energy is a concept similar to that of the others. However, this type of energy is or was approached in a more scientific manner, such as the following:
  - ○ Ethereal Energy is the driving force where the motion of planets and stars can move throughout the ether, like how a log can be moved by a flowing river.
  - ○ Ethereal Energy is thought to move in a vortex pattern to provide the least amount of resistance within a broad spectrum of frequencies.
  - ○ Physical matter is thought to be condensed Ethereal Energy.
  - ○ Ethereal Energy can be accumulated and transferred to other objects via resonance, much in the same way we can be tuned to a particular frequency on the radio and experience the sound through resonance. This concept was highly regarded among some great scientists, particularly Nikola Tesla and John Worrel Keely.
- 1930s: Wilheim Reich, a German psychiatrist, developed a pseudoscientific concept called Orgone Energy, a universal life-force similar to Animal Magnetism and the Odic Force.

The studies, beliefs, practices in these periods are mere glimpses into Cosmic Energy. There are many other cultures that are aware of Cosmic Energy, such as, but not limited to, West Africa and their Nyama, Russia and their Aura, the Mayans and their Ch'ulel, the Aborigines and their Alcheringa, and so on. It is a worldwide phenomenon. However, it seems as if, even though the majority of the world, even within Christianity, are aware of this energy, not as many strive to pursue the science behind its chemical makeup or attributes or its spiritual implications and so on. A concept forty thousand years or more older than Christ is still, unfortunately, slipping through the cracks.

Fortunately for us, the concept of Cosmic Energy is still alive in practices, including yoga, meditation, alchemy, shamanism, paganism, witchcraft, and many sciences (with prevaricate and elusive approaches). You don't have to be righteous. You don't have to be evil. You don't have to believe in any religion or conform to moral and ethical values. Like chaos, Cosmic Energy is in and around everything. It's awareness and particular physical and mental states that yield these energetic results. There are tools out there at your disposal (I'll present some of those later.), if needed. But pursue it on your own accord and in your own way.

CHAPTER I

An Origin Story, Its Fate, and Loke

B efore their geographical dispersion, there was a singular culture or race of people commonly referred to as Germanic. They took up what is now known as Germany as well as the Netherlands and Scandinavia. These Germanic people were Pagan, and when their beliefs eventually transformed to Norse theology, postdispersion and during the Viking era, their paganism was a veritable belief system, consummated with nine realms of the universe, the universal life-force accompaniment, gods and goddesses and social or existential levels of gods and goddesses, rituals and ritual sacrifices, celebrations and traditions, and so on.

Peculiarly, the stories of the gods and goddesses and their ultimate fate, as well as the fate of the world and the universe, share a common figure. The majority who are aware of the stories, to a limited extent, would assume that I'm referring to Odin or Thor, perhaps Heimdall or Freya. On the contrary, I'm referring

to Loki or Loke (Norske form). Loke is featured in so many of the ups and downs of the stories concerning the gods and goddesses and, usually, when it's a more imperative tale. You can easily corroborate this observation by reading the tales yourself. However, I will provide a brief account with Loke as our compass:

As we know, Loke often challenges the status quo, in regard to societal expectations and the laws of nature. In addition, Loke is also the mother of Sleipnir, Odin's eight-legged horse, to whom Loke gave birth after shapeshifting into a mare and courting the stallion Svadilfari, as described in the tale of The Fortification of Asgard.

In the tales, Loke is portrayed as a scheming, slightly cowardly trickster who cares only for shallow pleasures and self-preservation. He's mostly playful, malicious, and helpful. However, he can also be irreverent and nihilistic.

For example, in the tale of The Kidnapping of Idun, Loke winds up in the hands of a ferocious and angry giant, Thiazi, who threatens to kill Loke unless he brings him the goddess Idun. Loke complies in order to save his own life and, then, finds himself in the less than gratifying position of being threatened by the gods with death, unless he rescues Idun. He agrees to this request for the same reason as before, shapeshifting into the form of a falcon. He then carries the goddess back to Asgard in his talons. Thiazi pursues him desperately in the form of an eagle, but having almost caught up with Loke as he nears his destination, the gods light a fire around the perimeter of their fortress. The flames catch Thiazi and burn him to death, while Idun and Loke reach the halls of the gods safely. Loke ultimately comes to the aid of the gods, but only to rectify a calamity for which he himself is responsible. This theme is repeated in numerous and, as I said before, imperative tales.

After Thiazi's death, the giant's daughter, Skadi, arrives in Asgard and requests indemnity for the slaying of her father. One of her demands is that the gods make her laugh, something which only Loke is able to do. To accomplish this, he ties one end of a rope to the beard of a goat and the other end to his testicles. Both Loke and the goat screech as one pulls one way and the other pulls toward the opposite direction. Eventually, he falls over in Skadi's lap, and the giantess cannot fight the urge to laugh at such a foolish demonstration. Once more, Loke comes to the aid of the gods, but simply by being childish and outlandish, not by accomplishing any feat that anyone would have found to be honorable.

Any harm or inconvenience Loke may have caused the gods was always rectified, and he brought them many conveniences too. Sadly, he'd realized that, in a sense, they were beneath him. He regularly ran circles around them, lifting them up and taking them down. The implications were seemingly endless. He began to hate them. His disgust grew, and as it grew, so did the severity of his mischief. He began to question why these gods were worshipped in the first place and, ultimately, decided that they were unworthy of our praise. You can witness this transformation firsthand by reading the tales, like watching a smile turn to a frown.

He would soon make the decision to break away from the Aesir and have three more children, monstrous, vile children: the giant serpent, Jormungandr; the giant wolf, Fenrir; and Hel, a half-beautiful, half-morbid, rotting, and altogether repellent female humanoid who became the ruler of Helheim, realm of the dead. He eventually tricked the god, Hod, into inadvertently killing one of the most beloved gods in Asgard, Baldur. This treachery marked the beginning of Loke's descent into darkness and the change in the tides of a, more or less, stable universe or multiverse.

He transformed into a raven and went home to Jotunheim: realm of the giants. There, he told the giants that it was time to build the ship, Naglfar, a ship that will, one day, sail to Asgard on the day of Ragnarok, the end of days. Then he flew to another realm and transformed into a lizard, stirring up more plans for the demise of the gods. Finally, he settled on Earth (Midgard) and transformed into a salmon.

The salmon (Loke) swam in a stream when, after many, many restless nights and tireless searching, the gods found the stream and dragged a net through the water to catch him. The net, however, proved to be useless, and it was the great god Thor who caught Loke with his bare hands and forced him to return to his original form.

For all of his crimes against the Aesir and many others, the gods sewed Loke's lips shut and turned Loke's son, Vali, into a wolf that, in turn, killed Loke's other son, Narfi. The gods then forged a chain from Narfi's entrails and tied Loke to three rocks in that cave deep in the underworld.

A venomous serpent sits above him and drips poison onto Loke's face and chest. His proper wife, Sigyn, sits at his side with a bowl to catch the venom. But, soon, the bowl is too full, and Sigyn has to dump the poison. As a result, the poison hits Loke, occasionally, and he writhes in agony. In this state, he remains until breaking free at Ragnarok, the end of days, of all things.

Most of what we know about Germanic or Norse beliefs and practices comes from Tacticus's work, *Germania*, as well as the Eddas, the Icelandic Sagas, and skaldic verse and poetry. The Eddas are the primary source, compiled by the Icelandic scholar, lawspeaker, and historian Snorri Sturluson. Before the Eddas, all that was known of the Norse belief system was condensed to the stories of the more popular gods, such as Odin, Thor, Baldur, and the like. It wasn't until Snorri's contributions that we had a greater understanding of the belief system on a more accomplished level. Therein lies a dilemma: Snorri Sturluson was himself a Christian.

Fortunately for us, careful research with multiple credible sources will shed light on Snorri's Christianity, the state of things in Iceland during that time, and how a once-Germanic pagan belief transformed into a Norse belief system and, eventually, into a possible, somewhat tainted, Norse-Christian hybrid. Let's look at what we know about Snorri, his family, and their time and life in Iceland during the timeframe in question:

- Following Icelandic law after the year 1016, Christianity became the only legal religion in Iceland, and the penalty for breaking this law was a three-year exile. As a result, claiming that Snorri and other scholars during this time were Christian is debatable. In fact, numerous sources state that Snorri's nephew and other family members were actually publicly accused and tried for being followers of Odin.

- Skaldic poems and the tales within the Eddas were well known among all inhabitants and, before Chrisitan laws, were outwardly sung and spoken. To alter any of those highly regarded narratives would mean excessive punishment by his peers and fellow man.
- Snorri was the highest regarded historian for the Middle Ages. To overstate history as such a historian would be his professional and personal undoing.

However, there is a cause-and-effect sort of outlook on why Snorri's accounts may have been Christianized, and among most theologians, mythologists, and scholars who consort with and study Germanic paganism and Norse belief, this is regarded as the most likely scenario:

- In order to publicize his works, Snorri would have to translate, transform, and alter them to fit into the Christian worldview. Otherwise, they'd surely be destroyed, and he'd be exiled or worse.
- Christianity was already a formidable force in Iceland long before he was born. It is possible that the Christian alterations of Snorri's contributions were made long before he even existed.
- The demonizing of Loke and the concept of Ragnarok are viewed as being a direct result of Christian influence and requirements of Christian law, as they weren't extant before the works of Snorri Sturluson in any predating records.

Considering the aforementioned and weighing the sources, in all rationality, Christianity did have an effect on the Norse belief system. However, the majority of Snorri's works, as far as what we know from Roman accounts and other cultures around that time, as well as what we know of the politics and social behaviors from inside and outside sources, and the practices of the Germanic peoples and all that they entail, scarcely had anything to do with the Christians and was more or less devoid of any Christianity.

The incentive behind this chapter is personal. But it is, additionally, international and universal in and of itself. It's personal because I am a Vitki and Ergi-Norn by genetic authority and by family tradition. Knowledge of Germanic paganism and Norse belief is a prerequisite to becoming an initiate of either. The chapter is international in the same right. Finally, this chapter is universal or multiversal because these practices mean being part of the essence or foundation, something that predates human knowledge, something that holds dear the practices that came long before Christianity and many other belief systems, and it's one of the oldest primary tools to pursue the truth and the manipulation of Cosmic Energy, resulting in, as revealed before, achievement of enlightenment, connection with supreme consciousness or intelligence, complete self-awareness, maintenance of universal balance, to better shape individual destiny and ultimate outcome throughout the multiverse, and so on. I take pride in this, and perhaps in the future, if you don't already, you will too.

On Reverent Amalgam

All things considered, there is something "Wyrd" about the tangled web that is the coexistence of the Norse belief system, Christianity, and even Roman and Greek belief systems, as well as Zoroastrianism, Jewish mysticism, and so on. Every system has its expansion pack, and there are those who love it and endure and those who think they're fine the way they are and need not be changed. However, change is going to happen whether we like it or not, as I asserted earlier in this manuscript. It's unavoidable and steadfast. It's Chaos.

Reverent amalgam doesn't necessarily mean harmony, initially. In fact, the attributes of reverent amalgam can be synonymous with chaos, in that all things can be formed, then broken and rebuilt, reborn, stronger, better, faster, and so on. Eventually everything coincides. Even in matters of constant conflict, the conflict itself becomes commonplace, easy and rife with contour to those who endure it on a systematic level.

Consider the German rye (modest tomfoolery implied): We have relatively simple ingredients, rye flour, yeast, water, salt, sometimes sourdough culture, and so on, and these ingredients aren't particularly appetizing or appealing as they are individually. They may even clash, if combined improperly, resulting in nothing more than complete disaster. But with the right portions, combined properly, and with the perfect temperature to induce that ideal chemical reaction, the result is a strong and sophisticated assembly from which the masses will benefit for centuries.

Such is the case for reverent amalgam. It may happen peacefully and naturally at times, but in most cases, this type of amalgam is an end result of struggle and conflict, chaos, a chemical reaction, in a sense, that painfully breaks down the involved constituents until they're all part of a refined, tempered, singular unit.

This process and its manifestation is, with many collateral damages, precisely the process and ultimate outcome of Germanic paganism and the Norse belief system. Yes, Snorri was murdered as were countless other Scandinavians, Anglos, Celts, and basically a substantial percentage of every culture in the world to make it so. But it was not in vain, and now we have a developed, fruitful belief system and tool, and a flawless example of the aforementioned essence and/or foundation.

Not only did the Norse belief system survive its splice, complete with all its demands, but also it flourished. With what is known as Asatru, those awesome men and women that make up Grimfrost, those who individually practice the ways of the Vitki, Seithr, and Galdr, and the Pagans, Wiccans, certain National Socialist movements, and so on who study, practice, and incorporate it into their systems, the Norse belief system is more powerful than ever before.

The Satan, Loke

The Satanic Order av Wyrd (SOW, as in to sow the seeds of fate) is no exception, in respect to those who incorporate the Norse belief system and its practices, and we too have our own views on the process and the results of its amalgam as well as the implications of the amalgam's virtual ingredients. In fact, from the ways of the Vitki and Norns, Seithr and Galdr, to Yggdrasil and the nine realms, and the ways of Wyrd and Orlog, we here in SOW will attest that our order's core beliefs and practices are predominately those of the Norse belief system. But we'd be remiss if we didn't recognize our own personal ontogenesis: The Satan, Loke, his symbolic attributes and their ramifications, and his vital significance to universal existence.

The title of this chapter and the amalgam's constituents are simple and covered in bulk within the first introduction of this manuscript: Satan isn't Satan's name. Satan is a position or title meaning "the accuser" or "the adversary," and there are ancient Hebrew scriptures that predate the Bible that state in specific detail that there have been multiple fallen angels and rulers of hell, some of whom still serve God. That being said, due to the components that make up this amalgam, primarily composed of Germanic Paganism, the Norse belief system, the Roman belief system, and Christianity (Christianity also being an amalgam of Zoroastrianism, Judaic sects, the zodiac and Pagan sun worship, as well as ancient Egyptian theology, and so on), we, as the people who follow the system, can freely dub Loke Satan via definition, position, and association. There have been many and, if anyone deserves the appellation, within this realm where angels and demons, vaesen and fae, gods and goddesses, prophets and apostles, demigods and daevas, and so on exist (whether it be folkloric or literal), it's Loke.

Supporting Arguments
- Loke predates Christianity and associated sects and therefore, through seniority and by divine right as well as an inadvertent implicit election via reverent amalgam and Christian orthodoxy, the first and utmost merited Satan.
- Like the Satans who succeeded him, Loke is the nemesis of the All-father and those relevant, and he's the bringer of Ragnarok, the apocalypse.
- According to certain anecdotes, Loke, like certain comparable tales of Samael (a Talmudic, Gnostic, and Jewish mystical Satan), Loke condones the sins of man and often prefers to instigate tension and tragedy among mankind and gods alike.
- Loke's attributes fully correspond to those of the Satans (and one Satan, in particular, who has consistently been referred to as the

father of lies) in that he is generally characterized as the god of mischief and lies, destroyer of gods, and bringer of the apocalypse.

We'll provide copious testimonies toward the justification of our assertions, if needed. But the preceding arguments speak volumes and should assuredly suffice. Our logic is sound, our deeply held beliefs firm, and our resolve absolute!

Tangentially, within all belief systems exists symbolism for or representations of multiple facets including, but not limited to, the gods and goddesses themselves. Furthermore, many of those gods, goddesses, deities, and the like serve specific purposes, in the universe or solely on Earth, that may also be symbolic of themselves. For example, the New Testament Christian God is a symbol of peace and love; and love and peace are symbols of God. Other symbols associated with this Christian God are Alpha and Omega, the cross, the ichthus, and, more often than not, the star of David. (However, we here in SOW would much prefer the name and the implications of the seal of Solomon to that of the star of David).

To the Satanic Order av Wyrd, our Satan, Loke, has multiple symbols, and he represents multiple features of existence.

The Satan, Loke, Represents

- chaos and the universe (by proxy), in that he travels the paths of both obedience and malevolence, he builds and destroys carelessly and relatively effortlessly, and he's the bringer of the apocalypse;
- death and rebirth, for the very same reasons;
- evolution, in that he is a shapeshifter and can adapt to any situation and/or environment;
- mischief, malevolence, and evil, wrath, and revenge;
- playful nonsense;
- procreation and polysexuallity, in that he has had multiple partners of multiple species, genders, and realms, and has fathered (and mothered) many different species and genders;

- intelligence, in that he's calculative in all endeavors, providing solutions and solving even the most complex hardships;
- nature, his mother is of unknown origins and thought, in many learned factions, to be the Earth itself or Earth mother herself; and
- fire, in that he is thought to be a fire god, sharing similar names and their meanings as Loge and Lodur, fire gods or spirits who might actually be Loke himself.

Symbols of the Satan, Loke

- The Serpent: The Urnes Snake design consists of two snakes intertwining and swallowing each other's tails. Its origin falls on the entrance to the twelfth-century Urnes Stave Church in Ornes, Norway, as well as Germanic Pagan Broches dating back to the Iron Age. Despite many alleged Lokean amateur views, this design presumably is not linked to Loke. However, it has been thought to be associated with Jormungand, the giant world serpent, one of Loke's children. Therefore, many use the connection to Jormungand to justify its connection to Loke. Regardless, the serpent in general is a very appropriate symbol for Loke, in that it has long been an internationally recognized symbol of evil. The serpent can also represent Loke's ability to slither and shapeshift his way out of complex dilemmas. Loke's association with serpents doesn't stop at Jormungand, as the poisonous serpent that drips its venom on Loke from above (the story of Loke, Baldur, and Ragnarok) is also an acceptable relation.
- Fire: Loke has often been known as a fire god. Aside from the implications cited earlier, the artifact known as the Snaptun Stone is thought to convey an image of Loke's face with his lips sewn shut. This stone was used to protect the bellows from the heat of a blacksmith's forge. Therefore, fire is once more associated with Loke.
- The Gnezdovo amulet and the Bitterstad amulet: These amulets are thought to depict Loke as well. They may be used to pay homage to

Loke and are sold in abundance over the internet. If you're inclined to pay homage with these, I recommend Grimfrost, as they support the Norse cause more than the majority.

- The Salmon: The salmon is another symbol of Loke, as he transformed into a salmon when hiding from the gods following his treachery and murder of Baldur.

Why Loke?

There are many reasons why people worship gods. The three most popular reasons may or may not be evident. Regardless, the more popular reasons why people worship gods and build religions around them are as follows:

- to explain natural and supernatural phenomena
- to instill moral and ethical values
- to have something to look forward to after death

Some of the not-so-popular, but still well-known, reasons why people worship gods are, more or less, self-serving, praise and rituals directed toward overcoming obstacles, such as abundant crops or success in general, security, revenge, the successes of love, and so on. Depending on how enveloped one can be within his or her belief or faith can determine whether these praises are solely conscious or both conscious and subconscious. Evidently, the results of said praises widely vary for a number of reasons.

In addition, there are numerous cultures that favor certain gods or goddesses, or both, over other gods and goddesses within a singular belief system. This is what we call monolatry, and it's inevitable (with considerably infinitesimal variables). For example, the Christians, as a whole, that is to say, between Catholics, Protestants, Judaic systems, and the like, their primary focuses for worship are directed toward God or Yahweh, Jesus, Mary (mother of Jesus), and the saints.

- The Jews pray to and worship Yahweh, the sacred name of God revealed to Moses. They see Jesus as just another man, most likely a preacher, who lived during the Roman occupation.
- The Protestants only pray to God, and the Bible is the only source of authority.
- The Catholics pray to Mary (mother of Jesus) and the saints.
- Those who call themselves, simply, Christians pray to and worship Jesus, as they see him as God's words in the flesh, an extension of God.
- Then there are those who, according to certain documentation, worship and pay homage to Satan. Many are unaware of this, but the Ophites (and corresponding groups) are the earliest of these and, because of the coaxing of Adam and Eve into eating the forbidden fruit, resulting in their divine knowledge and knowledge of the ultimate truth regarding the chaotic give and take of good and evil, which would, in turn, give us the same knowledge, these Ophites, or the Cult of The Serpent, respected and paid homage to Satan or the serpent or both.

Clearly, these examples are only a fraction of the otherwise ample case that is monolatry. However, with these minor examples we can determine that there are numerous, if not boundless, reasons why each religious sect would favor, praise, or worship certain gods or goddesses or demigods or saints, and so on, even in a religion (Christianity) that most people, namely the followers, would assume is a watertight, reinforced, juggernaut, with only God and Jesus manning the helm.

The Answer to the Question (and I Hope This Isn't Too Crass) "Why Loke?":

Now that we've addressed the natural occupation that is monolatry, we can move on; and it's simple, really, in the grand scheme of things, the answer to the question. It's the ideal package. With what Loke represents, as well as his ability to manipulate the gods and so much more at will, throwing his pearls before swine, so to speak, it's no wonder he'd become the universe's undoing. In this domain and entertaining its existence, who wouldn't follow in his precedent?

In addition, as I said before, Loke predates Christianity and associated factions and therefore, through seniority and by divine right, as well as an inadvertent implicit election via reverent amalgam and Christian orthodoxy, the first and utmost merited Satan; and Satan is the ideal choice because of what Satan represents: rebellion and the questioning and challenging of authority, indulgence in sin, as it leads to self-gratification and an overall well-being, that we have freedom of will and our fate may be formed by that of our choosing (orlog), that it is possible to reach our highest personal potential (if we take the necessary steps to make it so), and that man is just another animal, more often worse than those who walk on all-fours. Satan is "man living as his prideful, carnal nature dictates. The reality behind Satan is simply the dark evolutionary force of entropy that permeates all of nature and provides the drive for survival and propagation inherent in all living things" (Peter H. Gilmore).

The Satan, Loke, is all of this and more, meeting and exceeding all expectations demanded by Satanic criteria. Furthermore, he is the quintessential choice for humanists and creationist alike, in that he is ever present in this powerful reverent amalgam and, simultaneously, due to his nonpartisan prestige and, as stated previously, his determination that the gods are

THE SATANIC ORDER AV WYRD

THE SATANIC ORDER AV WYRD

unworthy of our praise, he plainly condones the technological and scientific progression of mankind. In fact, progression by any means that we deem necessary as a collective and individually would surely be beneficial to him in the future, especially if it means putting ourselves before the gods or God.

The implications as to why he'd condone our behaviors toward progression are quite possibly negative. However, our undoing and the carnage that will befall our world/universe is an inevitability, and we're powerless against it. Fortunately, there is a solution. Nevertheless, I'll revisit this discussion in an ensuing chapter.

Loke's Role in the Satanic Order av Wyrd

Loke's role in the Satanic Order av Wyrd is one of versatility, and the best way to describe our relationship would be to dichotomize, isolate, and expose. We've already uncovered two ways, to a degree, in which one could embrace Loke in a religious or spiritual nature: theistic reverence and the associated worship therein as well as the use of Loke as a representation or symbol. The use of Loke as a symbol can be applied to Atheism in very much the same way that Satan is applied to the popular faction, the Church of Satan. The third and final way that Loke can be received is that which contains both Theism and Atheism, the Agnostic approach.

Agnosticism is the view that the existence of God, of the divine or the supernatural, is unknown or unknowable. Agnosticism can be deceptive, as there are wavering variables and drifting biases that may be taken into account. For example, one may be Atheistic, yet be aware that his or her convictions could conceivably be wrong, giving way to the possibility that there may be a deity somewhere in the universe or multiverse. The same can be said for their literal opposition, that a Theistic, possibly even Christian, individual can be aware that his or her convictions could conceivably be wrong, giving way to the possibility that there may not be a deity or deities in any realm, food for the Earth, as it were; and there are so many fluctuations involved that they're nearly immeasurable. In a way, this is a perfect example of Loke and of chaos, and this is where we come in.

28

Although we hold dear the ways of the Norse belief system and all that they entail, from the practices of the Vitki and Norns, Seithr, and Galdr to the concept of Yggdrasil and the nine realms, and the ways of Wyrd and Orlog; and despite the fact that we embrace it and we practice it, that it's our foundation, our essence—and even though it's one of the greatest tools to activate and manage our individual Cosmic Energy, in the face of our idol, the Satan, Loke—we too are Agnostic. We are Agnostic because, unless cold hard evidence is provided or a universal, telepathic, transcendent understanding is achieved or a universal comparative vision occurs, no one knows exactly what the afterlife is or what it contains. To depend on literature or the message of a filtered system without the means of understanding not only its foundation but also the foundation's origin, even the cause of the origin itself, is extremely unsubstantiated.

Personally, even after all of my theological and philosophical research, when I died (not mutually exclusive to this manuscript and a very long story for another time and place) and was later revived, it was something entirely different from what I'd conditioned myself to suspect, even if it was just a glimpse and, quite possibly, a byproduct of my physical condition during that evening. Eventually, I would learn to neutralize myself and unlearn much of what I'd consumed. I would learn to know myself, unconditionally, before taking on the universe or multiverse.

Nevertheless, until we relinquish life and until we are acquainted with universal and omnipotent truth, we will uphold our fealty to the Satan, Loke, and all that he represents and symbolizes, and we will continue to practice all that we practice in accordance with all that the Satanic Order av Wyrd represents and strives to achieve.

For Your Consideration or Those to Be Admitted

To many who live their lives outside the realm of religion, even those who predominantly live outside the realm of spirituality (and everyone else), the contents of this manuscript, thus far, may be perceived as marginally eccentric, even outright preposterous, and, if nothing else, essentially esoteric. Of course, that response, by most means, is arguably relatable, and we have no intention of enlisting the Atheists. They're doing quite well on their own. Nevertheless, we wouldn't be forthcoming if we didn't admit that SOW has a response to this party:

Corresponding to the Atheistic Satanic organization, the Church of Satan, the Atheist can view the Satan, Loke, as a symbol that represents self-worth, individualism, and enlightenment (in various facets), and as a representation of defiance against the Judaic faiths and their extensions (Christianity) as they suppress the true nature of humanity; and if Germanic Paganism and the Norse belief system remained unscathed, that is to say, free of Christian influence, they too would be an apt opposition against these Judaic faiths and their allies. Alas, they are not. But the Satan, Loke, is. In a sense, as a moderate afterthought, one could say that the Satan, Loke, alone is the cleansing agent in our amalgam, as he represents the rejection of every constituent within the compound.

Regardless, this symbolism and the implicit merger that would surely ensue is beneficial to the Atheist, in that their Christian opposition is the largest religion in the world and Christianty's most powerful antithesis are those of Satanic distinction. In other words, to extend one's reach is to extend one's prowess and expansion is the inevitable means to greatness. If the Atheists already have the very fruitful apparatuses that are the sciences and mathematics, our contribution is as follows: we are the first line of defense against that massive opposing force that is Christianity, if necessary, the eclipse to their sun or the sword to their looming fatal wound, so to speak. Yes, the Atheist could adopt any Satanic faction in this *hypothetical situation*. But why start at the end when they can start at the beginning?

Of course, we welcome anyone who can wholly connect with our goals, our views, and are ready and willing to apply it all when the time is suitable. We haven't addressed our goals and views or their practical applications in full. However, this will be revealed in the next article.

CHAPTER II

Our Views and Their Practical Applications—Section I

The Concept of Yggdrasil and the Nine (10) Realms

Yggdrasil is the central and colossal sacred ash tree, recounted by Snorri Sturluson in the Poetic and Prose Eddas, and it connects all nine (10) realms of the cosmos. The realms exist at the branches and roots of Yggdrasil, and there are myriad creatures that exist around and inside this world tree.

The Nine (10) Realms

- Midgard: the realm of humanity
- Asgard: the realm of the Aesir, the highest class of the gods
- Vanaheim: the realm of the Vanir, the lower class of the gods
- Jotunheim: the realm of the Giants
- Niflheim: the primordial realm of Ice
- Muspelheim: the primordial realm of fire
- Alfheim: the realm of Elves
- Svartalfheim: the realm of the Dwarves
- Helheim: the realm of the of dead

See diagram on next page.

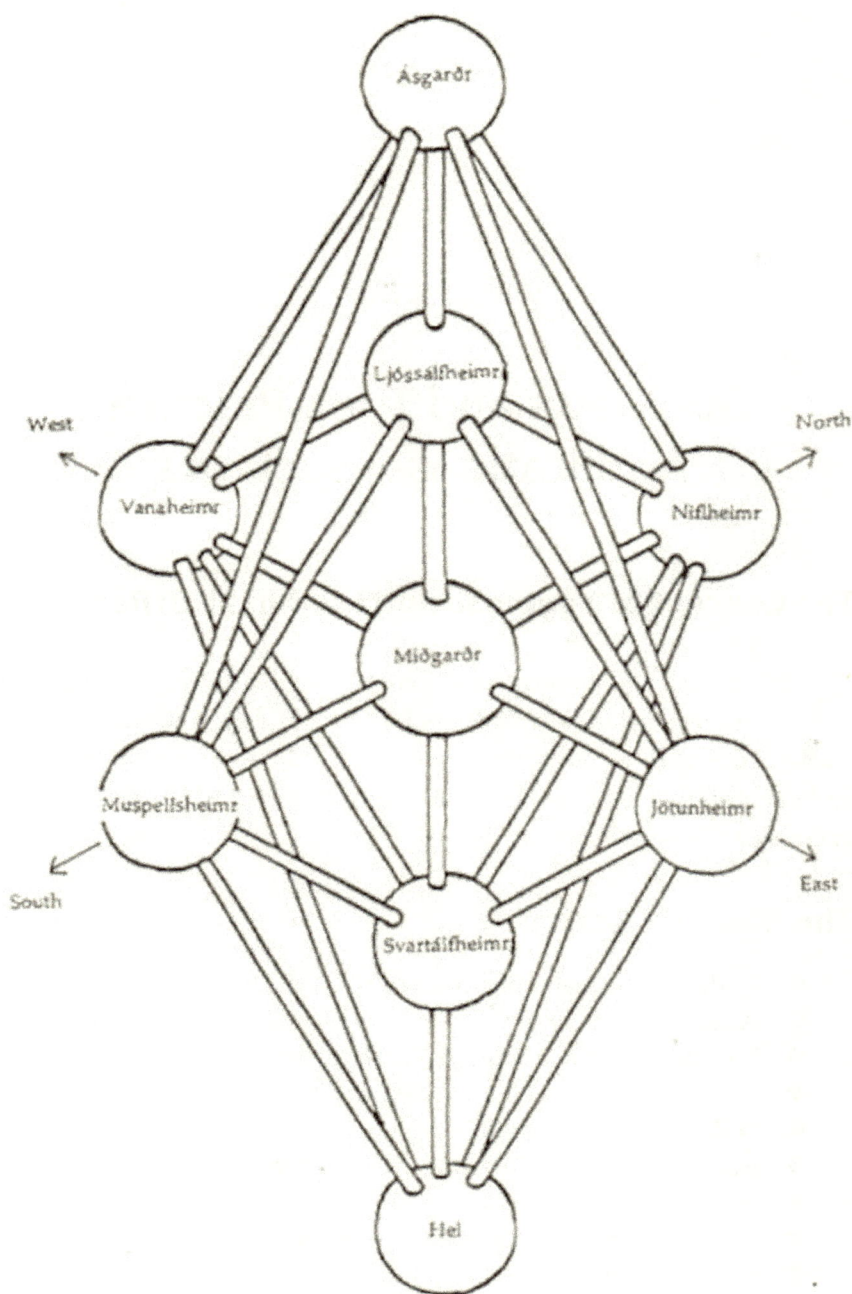

However, there is one more realm, a realm highly regarded, yet no one ever seems to step forth to address the issue, that this, the realm of the primordial void, where the fires of Muspelheim and the ice of Niflheim collide in a massive black void of pure chaos and vacuous darkness. Ginnungagap is a realm, in itself, a tenth realm with the power of creation of anything, anyone, anywhere it deems necessary. To reject this realm as a legitimate realm, to be included in the literary works of the past and the diagrams and maps of Yggdrasil and the Nine Realms today, is sophomoric. After all, this is where we derive our Wyrd, eventually see the Wyrd, and ultimately manipulate Orlog and, consequently, Wyrd itself.

Seithr and Galdr/Wyrd and Orlog Command: Applied to Cosmic Energy

Seithr is the Viking shamanistic practice of realizing the course of fate, via Wyrd, and working within its system to create change (Orlog). Seithr often includes in its practices, trance states of consciousness (psychedelic mushrooms being an integral multifaceted tool), and astral projection. Chanting is also an essential part of Seithr, whether it be to evoke certain gods or goddesses, call on the power of specific runes, to charm/curse, and so on, and this chanting is known as Galdr.

As stated in **Introduction Part IV: On Cosmic Energy**, there are numerous reasons why tapping into Wyrd and developing your Orlog is beneficial: achievement of enlightenment or universal truth and/or connection with supreme consciousness or intelligence, complete self-awareness, maintenance of universal balance, nourishment of body cells and the support of internal organs and their functions, and promotion of happiness and general well-being, and so on. It's what many call a no-brainer, and it is a crucial part of the Satanic Order av Wyrd.

The following are some initial exercises to familiarize yourself with the processes that are Seithr. Starting with the first step, aligning with Yggdrasil. Yggdrasil is always the starting point for any Seithr journey.

What You'll Need

- Psilocybin psilocybin mushrooms (approximately 0.50 Kilogramskilograms)
- A a black ceremonial robe
- A a mat or blanket upon which is the Vegvisir surrounded by the elder futhark (drawn, painted, or printed)
- a drawing, painting, or print of the Web of Wyrd

Web or Wyrd (left), Vegvisir with Elder Futhark (right)

Aligning with Yggdrasil

Place the Web of Wyrd to the north of where you'll be standing. Place your mat or blanket on the floor, the top of the Vegvisir facing north. Place your mushrooms at the edge of the northern point of the mat.

Sit on the mat in a cross-legged position. Ingest the mushrooms. Close your eyes. Allow the body to settle so that the breath can relax into its natural quiet state. Once the body has settled, slowly move the abdomen out, drawing down the diaphragm, which will draw air into the lungs. To exhale, pull the abdomen in, which will expel air from the lungs. For a fuller exhalation, contract the ribs. The pace of deep breathing should be slow and rhythmic so that the inhale length matches that of the exhale.

Now, stand at the heart of the Vegvisir, facing north toward the Web, place your feet at shoulder width. Gaze into the Web of Wyrd. Envision your spine in line with the center stave of the Web, your feet being placed on the outer staves. Do not lock your ankles or knees. Your entire body should be as relaxed as it can be without collapsing so that you can bend and contour with the flow of Wyrd.

Continue to gaze upon the Web. Breathe in deeply and exhale entirely. Feel your feet sink into the floor. Feel the bottom of your feet where they touch the floor. Feel the air surrounding you, any insignificant gust of wind, noticed. Hear every sound.

Close your eyes. Envision roots, extending from the top of your crown, through your body, to the bottom of each foot and out the bottom of your feet, moving down through the Vegvisir, the floor, into the earth and through the layers of the earth.

Move your less dominant foot ever so slightly. Feel the root extending out from the ball of your foot, sinking through the layers of earth, until it touches a spring-fed pool. Feel the warm, damp sediment, layer upon layer as your root sinks deeper into the well spring. This sediment is the Orlog, the layers of primal law, all of the circumstances, choices, and actions that came before you and are happening now. Your layer is on top, then your parent's layers and their parent's layers, all the way to the beginning of time.

The deeper this root goes, the colder the energy, the Wyrd, permeating everything, becomes. Follow the root as far as you can, until you come to the realm of ice, Niflheim. Urd is here, sampling the Wyrd and Orlog that flows all around. Absorb Urd's sample into your root. It gets warmer as it is absorbed and melts the ice around you forming another pool. There, the surface of the pool surrounds your root, feeling the tension of the water's surface. This is the place of Verdandi, the still point, the present moment. From here you can feel the past and see potential in the reflection of the pool. Breathe into the present moment and let your ego, your fears, and your expectations dissolve as you exhale.

As the energy enters through the bottom of your foot, look to see the third sister, Skuld, who shows you how to best direct your Orlog, as we create our layer in the well. This combined energy flows up your leg slowly, until it meets the perineum, the point between the destructive and creative forces. This is an energetic transfer point for our body and the body of Yggdrasil.

Now, let your consciousness cross to the opposite leg. Feel it move slowly down the inside of your dominant leg. Let it sink. Invision the root extending from this foot that sinks down, until it touches the water, the well of Mimir. Let this root rest on the pool's surface. As your root begins to sink into the well of pondering, your understanding of your Orlog becomes clearer. Odin's eye is in this well. Mimir's head is in this well. Let your root sink below the surface of the water, far enough to absorb the wisdom that belongs to you. As you sink this root deeper, the energy becomes warmer still and connects to the fires of Muspelheim.

Feel the heat rising up your root. Feel the root touching the well of Mimir. Feel it rising up your toes, ankle, shin, calf, knee, thigh, and up to the perineum.

Now, squeeze your buttocks together while breathing in. Then release. Feel the power point of the perineum, the point between your reproductive and destructive forces. It is from this point that a third root extends. Bounce, slightly, as though you are sitting on horseback. The root from your perineum moves down and touches the floor. This is the third root, the third leg of a tripod. These are the three points that create your lane of existence, a sacred triangulation.

Sink your perineum root through the layers, as before. Imagine a coin shaped blackness surrounded by ice on one side and fire on the other, corresponding to the feet that these elements were assigned before. This space is called Ginnungagap, the void. Feel your perineum root search for nourishment. Breathe in deeply. Hold it. As you exhale, feel the root move into Ginnungagap. It touches steam, ice, and water. This water is boiling as the realms of ice and fire collide. This is the primordial well of creation, Hvelgelmir, the place of the primordial serpent, Nidhogg. This serpent that gnaws and feasts upon our tap root, the depository of the dead that would be reborn, is the void of everything and nothing, all at once.

Bring the energy of your tap root slowly upward, until it reaches the perineum once more. You three roots are aligned with the roots of Yggdrasil. The negative charge of ice, Urd's well, the positive charge of fire, Mimir's well, and Ginnungagap, the black void of infinite chaos, destruction, and creation, Hvelgelmir. Your three roots create your pyramid. Your spine becomes a beam of darkness, surging from the tip of the pyramid, upward.

Squeeze your buttocks together yet again. Feel the three roots connected at the point of the perineum. Bring the energy from each root up your spine. The tap root energy moves up through the center of your spine like the marrow therein. It nourishes each vertebra, mixing with the synovial fluid, bringing vitality back to your marrow. It rises slowly to rest at the occipital ridge. The energies from your left and right foot begin to travel up the spine, in a spiral, spiraling your core root, the perineum root. They travel up the core like snakes on the caduceus. They cross at the energetic points throughout your body, chakras, if you will. Your spine and the trunk of Yggdrasil are unified through this braid of energy from the roots. Breathe in as the spirals move up your spine. Ice and fire combine to create a malleable frost, the element of creation, caused by the interaction between the two elements, and it tempers the roots. As the spiral moves up your spine, feel how it affects your stomach, diaphragm, heart, and throat. Let the movement of this root energy move the energy in those spaces.

These energies meet at the base of your skull where the spine and skull connect, your brain stem. This is the place where the branches of Yggdrasil and yourself begin to grow. Let the tip of your tongue rest between your two front teeth. The little bump between them is the energy transfer station on the top of your tree, of you. It is the mirror of the perineum. The three middle realms exist between these two points.

Feel the energy from the perennial root, Hvergelmir moving up into your reptilian brain, the oldest part of your brain. Here, the ancestor memory is stored. It moves up through the pineal gland, where meditation and enlightenment happen. It moves up and over your skull, falling down upon you like rain.

Feel the energy of Urd's well running up the right side of your brain, the second oldest part of your brain complex. It engages the ancient centers of right-brain functions and allows ancestor memory to play out in dreams. It shows us the Web of Wyrd, in its entirety. It is the second branch of the tree.

Feel the energy of Mimir running up the left side of your brain, where pondering and linear linking are engaged. The fires of invention, speech, mathematics, and the great epiphanies are generated here. The left and right brain are connected by the corpus callosum, the latest development of the human brain. These branches of your tree create a network of communication that allows us to engage our whole brain at once. They are nourished by the mist of Hvergelmir and the drizzle of the energy of creation. Feel your scalp tingle, as the rain of energy drops gently, yet abruptly, on your head.

Jut your chin up to the sky, open your mouth wide and stick out your tongue. Let the combined energy of the wells trickle into your mouth. Rest the tip of your tongue between your two front teeth and breathe in through your nose. Breathe in the waters of the wells as the branches convulse above.

Now stretch out your arms, palms up, to further catch the energized rain. Breathe in deeply. Fill your palms with the Wyrd/Orlog/energy and let that energy overflow, running down your arms and trunk. Feel it running down your legs, through the roots of your feet and back into the wells. You are a complete circuit of this energy, you are Yggdrasil.

' Lower your arms, roll your shoulders, and move your body parts and extremities, loosely. If your eyes are closed, open them, and feel yourself fully in the present moment. Breathe slowly and know that you have aligned yourself with Yggdrasil. You can now manipulate your Orlog at will. Eventually, you'll also see Wyrd clearly, making navigation and manipulation throughout and of the Wyrd an effortless task.

More Tools for Ritual Purposes

- a gandr or wand
- a drinking horn
- An an offering bowl
- A a ritual carving knife and dagger or blade

Further Seithr rituals primarily include astral projection, for a number of purposes, including, but not limited to, cosmic knowledge, entrance into alternate realms, prophecy, personal development and well-being, tranquility, communion with alternate entities or gods, goddesses, or ancestral entities (or some combination of these), discovering your Cosmic Mate, healing the self or others, freedom from the ego, a new appreciation of life, etc. This practice gives testament to the concept of Cosmic Energy, and is supported by myriad of scientists, pseudo-scientists, professors of numerous fields, shamans, and a large number of practitioners from all over the world, not unlike the cultures I'd previously listed in Introduction Part IV: "On Cosmic Energy."

During astral projection, in theory, there is a connection between the astral body and the physical body so that you can return when you are ready. This connection is referred to as the silver cord. The silver cord is similar to that of an umbilical cord that tethers the astral body so that it can return to the physical body.

In the *Journal of the American Society for Psychical Research*, professors and scientists issued a report about a woman who had out-of-body experiences. The researchers studied the physiological data while she was sleeping and found that her out-of-body experiences happened when she was in a nonawake, nondreaming stage of brain wave activity. The alpha activity of the brain was slowed and there was no indication of activation within the autonomic nervous system.

Other evidence of astral projection occurs when a person has been medically tested as non-responsive, unconscious, or declared clinically dead. In these instances, doctors said that the body was unresponsive, but after waking, the patient was able to share details about the events that ensued in the room. While the body was unresponsive, astral projection made it possible for them to observe the other people in the room, as well as the procedures that were completed.

The truth is that scientists can only measure the physical responses that are happening within the body, there is not a way to measure the astral experiences that occur, at least not yet. But we are converging on corresponding technology. Science can't fully explain all aspects of astral projection at this point, and much of the information on the topic is based on personal experience and anecdotal evidence. As a result, astral projection is considered to be a pseudoscience.

Regardless of its credibility in certain circles, astral projection is an intrinsic practice for SOW and those who practice Seithr. The following example is the most successful method for astral projection, the SOW Method:

The SOW Method-Astral Projection

The goal of the SOW Method is to put your body into an inactive or sleep state, while your mind, on the other hand, remains attentive or awake. It is extremely difficult to do this if you are in a place where disturbances may occur. Find a secure and peaceful location. You want to do this at dusk as well. Once these terms have been met, very little is required moving forward.

Firstly, ingest 0.5 kilograms of your psilocybin mushrooms and wait for twenty minutes. While you wait, you'll need to wear your cloak. Lay down your Vegvisir mat (once again, the north point of the Vegvisir must face north). You'll need your offering bowl and your ritual dagger or blade. Place your offering bowl in front of the left stave nearest to the north or middle stave and place the ritual dagger or blade in front of the right stave nearest to the north or middle stave of the Vegvisir. Place a drawing of the rune, Eihwaz, in front of the north or middle stave.

The significance of this rune (aside from the fact that this is my rune, my everything) is that it is symbolic of Yggdrasil as well as the union between the domains of life and death, protection from complications, and the gateway of transformation. Being that Yggdrasil is what connects us, so to speak, to the other realms of the universe and the rune has the power and attributes that it has, we pay homage to Yggdrasil with a Blót, and use Eihwaz to do so with an offering of great importance: our life-force.

For a few minutes, we'll use Galdr to charge the rune. Sit at the heart of the Vegvisir, facing to the head of the north stave, and set the drawing of Eihwaz in your lap. Gaze upon it for a minute. Close your eyes. In a low, throaty voice recite this note (the pronunciation isn't absolutely imperative, but try your best):

Eihwaz Eihwaz Eihwaz
e e e e e e e e e (closed vowel sound)
iwu iwa iwi iwa iwu
iwo iwe iwi iwa iwu
e e e e e e e e e (closed vowel sound)

Repeat this incantation twice. Open your eyes. Set the rune back to its original location. Now take your ritual dagger or blade into your right hand and, as you cut sparingly into the palm of your left hand, recite this passage:

From here to there
And back again
With your sway
From here to there
And back again
Yet here my body stays
Take my blood
Set me free
I pay you homage
Take my blood
Give to me
Vast strength and knowledge

Set the ritual dagger or blade down to its original location. Let the blood collect in your palm, before pouring into your offering bowl. Dip the tip of your right index finger into the blood and dab the tips of points of Eihwaz, then the tips that follow those points. Set the offering bowl down to its original location.

Now, lay on your back with your head at the heart of the Vegvisir. You should already be relaxed. Free yourself from stress, worry, and physical discomfort. It might be helpful to tense up, then release your muscles. But as long as you are calm, still, and without distraction, you should be able to continue.

Move your physical body toward sleep. If you start to feel numb, this is fine. Do not attempt to keep your body awake. It is simply easy enough to lay, eyes closed, and to let your thoughts drift. When you start to lose physical sensations, you have reached your desired state.

Do nothing. "This isn't much of a method so far," you may be saying. It's true—it sounds like nothing is happening. Physically, you are not moving. You should begin to look at the darkness in front of your eyes. Some strange things can happen in this state. Your field of vision may feel like it increases, which is an odd but enjoyable sensation.

You may also notice light patterns and noise. It's safe to ignore them, as they will eventually disappear. At this stage, you may feel like you are falling, floating, or feeling and sensing absolutely nothing at all. Maintain this feeling. Continue laying and observing.

You will reach the vibration state. This is a well-known effect within the astral projection phenomenon. It is a feeling of weightless disorientation, tingling, but with substance. Using willpower, you can enhance or decrease the feeling. It is extremely hard to describe in text and must be experienced firsthand to be understood.

Reaching this stage is a milestone. Once you reach this strange sensation, you will be more acclimated to it on future attempts. If, on your first attempt, you reach this vibration state, then count yourself very lucky.

One thing to remember about this stage is that there should be no rush. It took me a long time to understand that this vibration state can be maintained for a very long period of time. It is also very good for exploring your own thoughts and should be seen as the equivalent to a deep, introspective meditation. You can easily create vivid images that can be informative and entertaining in the vibration state. Images in your mind will appear much more vivid than usual.

When you reach the vibration stage, you want to enhance it. It will feel natural, even though you may have no idea what that means. Making the vibrations stronger will feel disorienting for a short while.

Once the vibration period dwindles, you should attempt separation. You can picture the vibration stage as the separation.Your consciousness is now in your astral body fully, but your astral body is still inside your physical self. You need to test the waters by moving a limb and another limb, and so on.

You should begin with an arm or a leg. invision your arm extending, that is to say, lengthening until it reaches something. You should try thIsaiah

Extend an arm and try to analyse the sensations. It might be helpful at this stage if you have an object nearby. Try to touch it. It is a strange sensation, mentally moving your body around. But the feeling becomes natural soon enough.

The main goal is a full, conscious separation. Once you have partially separated, you should attempt to disassociate yourself with your body. There are many ways to do thIsaiah

Imagine your body from a third person perspective, and it may spontaneously happen of its own accord. This is quite a powerful little technique, as it enhances the experience.

Another similar method here is to imagine yourself a few feet above your body. The link between your body and mind here is said to be very faint. Sense your sleeping body under you.

At this point, you should be freed from yourself, ready to travel as you please. I recommend the ten realms. They're exquisite.

***

Practice makes perfect and patience is a virtue. Cliché, I know. But nothing can be more appropriate. Tattoo these clichés on your brain and relish in their simplicity and beauty. You'll need it.

You may eventually begin to astral project with a mission. Arm yourself with fearlessness, attention to detail, and a sound mind. You'll want to ask the right questions, when the time and circumstances are appropriate. Nothing ruins a trip into the realms quite like a rude and playful god or goddess, or otherwise. I learned this the hard way.

CHAPTER III

Our Views and Their Practical Applications—Section II— Cosmic Energy: Science and Theory

N early identical to the concept highly regarded among great scientists, such as Nikola Tesla, John Worrel Keely, Victor Schauberger, and Wilhelm Reich, Ethereal Energy: Cosmic Energy, or Wyrd, in accordance with the beliefs of the Satanic Order av Wyrd, is the driving force, present in all living things and nonliving natural materials, where the motion of planets and stars, and everything in between, can move throughout the ether, like how driftwood can be moved by a flowing river. Cosmic Energy is thought to move in a vortex pattern to provide the least amount of resistance within a broad spectrum of frequencies. Physical matter is thought to be condensed Cosmic Energy. Cosmic Energy can be accumulated and transferred to other objects via resonance, much in the same way we can be tuned to a particular frequency on the radio and experience the sound through resonance.

Everybody has the ability to see the Cosmic Energy field that surrounds matter. We are born with this natural gift. Unfortunately, we have been brought up to focus only on so-called real material objects; visions of light and color surrounding people and in nature generally are dismissed as optical illusions. But it is possible to retrain yourselves to regain this ability through our alignment with Yggdrasil and other methods to be addressed in future text.

Cosmic Energy Frequencies

The human Cosmic Energy field contains numerous energy centers. Cosmic Energy is spiraling throughout these centers within these fields in a vortex fashion, thereby sustaining the field itself. Since Cosmic Energy is essentially contained within a broad spectrum of frequencies, the energy, once accumulated, can be transferred onto other objects by way of resonance through these frequencies. On a cosmic level, the same phenomenon exists. The elements, out of which our planet and everything on it is composed, all resonate to different cosmic frequencies and they each have their own specific eigenfrequency (individual intrinsic frequency). Therefore, the energy fields of objects and their color emanations differ according to their chemical composition. Therefore, numerous cells, organs and symbiotic organisms within us also resonate to different cosmic frequencies that combine with our own, creating an even more complex Cosmic Energy brand or caliber.

What does modern science think about energy frequencies that pervade space? Well, apart from the quantum energy that every atom contains, there are atmospheric resonance phenomena that have been investigated, called the Schumann waves or resonances. These are very long waves of extremely low frequency, which are present everywhere in the atmosphere on this planet. Schumann waves have been identified as part of the natural electromagnetic radiation, which is particularly important for life on this planet. The human brain actually resonates with these atmospheric waves. NASA has studied these Schumann waves extensively and recognized the importance of these waves for human health. Space shuttles are equipped with artificial Schumann wave generators to simulate the natural electromagnetic environment of the earth. In addition, Schumann wave researcher Dr. Phil Callahan has traveled all over the world measuring these frequencies. What he found was that most prehistoric monuments and church towers and, in particular, the round towers of Ireland act as dielectric antennas and amplifiers for Schumann waves, creating an enhanced natural electromagnetic environment within their vicinity. This explains the special atmosphere in churches and why people experience a feeling of reduced stress, ecstasy, reinvigoration, and so on.

The Satanic Order av Wyrd pays close attention to these frequencies and finds that Cosmic Energy is not just a phenomenon contained within a broad spectrum of frequencies that can be transferred and absorbed onto and by other objects by way of resonance. The Cosmic Energy fields that we emanate individually carry signatures or tethers, as they do within the concept of Orlog and Wyrd, that have their own special frequency levels and individual calibers that coincide with that of our ancestors. These energy fields, with their ability to reinvigorate and strengthen, empower, can do so, with unsurpassable success, through communion with those of similar or specific origin. If you are of multiple origins, genetically, then, to increase your chances of absorbing Cosmic Energy and, thereby, strengthening your own Cosmic Energy with great success, you would then partner with those who share the same genetic origins of your largest percentage. For long-lasting, meaningful relationships leading to procreation and ultimately offspring, and the repetition of this process, you will filter out the minor percentages of your genetic origins for future generations, your descendants, leaving them with fortitude and the convenience of being able to strengthen their Cosmic Energy fields in a more unconditional value.

This doesn't mean that other energies, belonging to different races, are weaker, per se. But I will admit that this subject is debatable. However, the only point that I'm projecting at this time is that different races will conflict with and dilute your most powerful eigenfrequency fraction (Don't shoot the messenger.), which leads us to the next section.

47

Social Darwinism and Racial Hygiene

Subsequently, as a result of our eigenfrequency findings, we've embraced the concepts of Social Darwinism and Racial hygiene. Evidently, these concepts are views that most discourage. But it is a necessary evil and beneficial on multiple levels, such as, but not limited to, as stated previously, strengthening and/or empowering our individual Cosmic Energy fields with greater success or precision, acknowledging our differences and embracing them results in self-gratification, pride in our origins, and a higher sense of being, avoidance of social degeneration (if applicable), and so on.

Racial hygiene isn't applied in the same manner as the Nazis, at least not to that extent. The eradication of any race to preserve racial purity is unnecessary. Antimiscegenation and the circumvention of meaningful, elongated relationships with dissimilar races within the Satanic Order av Wyrd is adequate enough. We won't try to keep people outside our Order from establishing such connections. However, within SOW, these regulations are strictly enforced.

As I said earlier, I'm not saying that the energy belonging to other races is weaker, per se. The only differences between us and them are energy signature and genetic material. You don't need to harbor hate or ill will toward them.

Unfortunately, with our deeply held beliefs, they're very likely to hate or fear us. This is natural and expected, and we are prepared. Part of being prepared on an individual level is maintaining reserves toward the opposing force(s) or others who differ genetically and energetically. This is ingrained in our culture(s) as part of evolution and rightly so.

Natural selection is ever present in nature as well as society. It is the key mechanism in evolution and expansion, without which neither could take place. Yes, in theory and in very few books written by dirty, hippie quacks, evolution without natural selection can occur. To those authors and theirs, I say pull your heads out of your asses and breathe some fresh air. If you still feel the same way that you did, prerectal exit, off yourselves. To forgo natural selection is to forgo adaptation, the close match between organisms and their environment, predators and their prey, flowers and their pollinators, first-, second-, and third-class citizenship, democracy, war, and so on. We would have no reason to do anything, no need to pursue bigger and better things, and a world like that is not only excessively boring, but unfathomable and asinine. In order to live in this hypothetical scenario, we'd require unlimited resources and no confrontation, no monogamous love-based intent toward anything, and so on. It's a fucking pipe dream.

The perpetuating force of natural selection in the human world (for the most part) is Social Darwinism, which emerged in Western Europe and North America in the 1870s and applied biological concepts of natural selection and survival of the fittest to sociology, economics, and politics. Those who have gained their higher incomes, higher social status, and general multifaceted power, individually and collectively, did so through intelligence, imagination, and determination; and, statistically, without question, those who flourished throughout history, in a myriad of ways, are those of the western world, the so-called white races. It's difficult to grasp, to accept. But it's the truth.

Professor of sociology and political scientist William Graham Sumner maintained, to a certain extent, that those of you who feel an obligation to provide assistance to those unequipped or underequipped to compete for resources, you will lead your country to a state in which the weak and inferior are encouraged to breed more like you or with you, as well as meddle in the affairs of things they know nothing about and are unable to comprehend, and this will eventually lead to your country's and its people's downfall or destruction. This statement is not only accurate on a political and economic, societal level, but also on the Cosmic Energetic level, and directly correlates with those of the western world, the white races. This ensuing degradation will not be on our hands and we will not be omitted, but considered by the powers that be, if and when that supreme opportunity presents itself, because we've undertaken crucial protocols to maximize our power, our knowledge inside and outside our material realm of existence, and so on. Become an asset, not a hindrance.

How to Protect and Empower Your Cosmic Energy Field

If you're sharing a passing conversation, shaking a hand, fighting, fuck-ing, or simply sharing a living space, you're exchanging energy through the aforementioned frequencies directly from your Cosmic Energy fields. This can have a negative effect and affect on your physical and emotional states. Depending on those with which you interact, even within relations regarding the same genetic origins (if the other person carries with them ill intent), the exchange may be more one-sided in their favor, you may absorb negative, self-destructive energy that will thrust you into failure on multiple levels, and it can leave you empty, powerless, ill (physically and mentally), and can even kill you.

Any of these varying types of energies are products of your physical and emotional state, and they're composed of the preordained signatures of your genetic origin. Fortunately, the Satanic Order av Wyrd views the negative, so-called self-destructive aspects of energy as being subjective. Negative and positive energies are subjective in the same way that the concept of good and evil is subjective. To reiterate, take a glimpse into the life of Angus Carlisle:

Wee Angus Carlisle was raised within a slightly organized, extremely violent, criminal razor gang, called the Billy Boys, in Glasgow, Scotland. Since before he could remember, Angus had witnessed savage murders, rape, drug and alcohol abuse, and so on. Many members of the Billy Boys kept their children in the dark, more or less, as to the goings on, regarding their misdeeds. Angus was an exception.

Angus's father had a special brand of darkness, one that didn't sheathe its intent, as did his father's father, and so on and so forth. The Carlisle family had its own family values and its own sophisticated approach to family matters, and they were happy, truly happy. Those of whom they trusted and loved never felt any sense of urgency or unrest. In fact, they felt safer and content, even slightly envious, but they were loyal. If you were on the opposite end, that is to say, if the Carlisles had adverse sentiments toward anyone, that person would meet an end in one of three ways: They would be killed before they could've anticipated its convergence. If they were aware of how a Carlisle felt, they would go mad in anticipation of the horrors to come, in which case, they'd usually commit suicide or try to run to no avail. Or they were tortured in unimaginable ways, physically, psychologically, and emotionally.

Angus had a relatively normal upbringing. He had many friends, many of whom confided in him and trusted him and sought him out for help in many facets. Any social activity he'd had, outside the family, was, for the most part, a familiar occurrence, as he did many of the same endeavors within his own home.

Angus was in his preteens when his father was apprehended by the police in their home. In that moment, Angus grabbed a cleaver from the kitchen, stealthily got the drop on two officers, beheading one and swiftly removing the face of the other, before being shot to death by the remaining officers.

In Angus's mind, he was doing the right thing. He was protecting his family against an oppressive, dare I say, evil posse. The police officers were the offenders or the villains, the opposing force or the axis, as it were.

This is why we consider the concept of good and evil or positives and negatives, within a necessary and reasonable context, to be subjective. If one is spawned and raised in darkness, and believes his or herself to be doing right by his or herself and his or her loved ones or acquaintances or associates, and so on, those who oppose him or her by way of righteousness are perceived to be the villain, the adversary, the axis.

As a result, due to the Satanic Order of Wyrd's devotion to Loke and our natural inclination to follow in his precedent, as well as our propensity of being exceedingly open to, in effect, nearly everything, we, as naturally dark, marginally malevolent creatures, welcome the adversity that negative energy provides. We overcome it and transform it into pure Cosmic Energetic power, because we don't see that darkness as darkness. That energy is just yet another angle in which we can bend and manipulate in ways we deem necessary, if necessary. In truth, nothing beats the special brand of darkness that we can provide.

The Satanic Order av Wyrd does not fear those who harbor ill intent, pertaining to the extortion of our Cosmic Energy fields, as we have protocols in place to circumvent such conduct. In fact, predominantly, we do not fear anyone or anything, in any occasion (to be addressed in a later chapter). Regardless, the following ritual will protect your Cosmic Energy field and allow for an effortless process of taking in or releasing your energy at will and at any given time.

Aegishjalmur or Helm of Awe (Above)

Lokean Armor

Ingest your mushrooms, same proportion as before. Remove your clothes. Sit at the heart of the Vegvisir. Wait twenty minutes. Fill your offering bowl in the same manner as before, your Vegvisir pointing north, bowl on the left, blade on the right.

Instead of Eihwaz, we're using the Aegishjalmur, or the Helm of Awe. You will paint this symbol over your pineal energy center, slightly above the eyes and centered on the forehead. This symbol is powerful, forming a sphere of authority that strikes overwhelming fear into the enemy, a representation of the serpent's ability to paralyze its prey before striking. It also invokes protection for those who bear it. In its center is the Sun Cross as well. This is a representation of the four seasons and a calendar of sorts. This can indicate the longevity of our ritual, in that you only need to perform it once a year, preferably on the full moon following the spring solstice, only once a year: the Aegishjalmur is that powerful.

You may use a paint brush, or something similar, and a mirror to apply the symbol. However, while applying, you will repeat this mantra until the symbol is complete.

Winter, Spring, Summer, Fall,
I hold dominion over all
who mean me harm, who think they've won.
I covet cabal.

Once you've finished applying your Aegishjalmur, close your eyes. View the images or shapes or light aberrations behind your eyelids.

Envision the Helm emerging from the other images or shapes or light aberrations. Focus on it. Make it the centerpiece of it all. Envision a sphere of luminescence growing from the helm, larger and larger, until you are encompassed by it.

Envision that sphere being filled, with every exhale, a black mist. Continue doing so, until the sphere is completely black, like a sphere of obsidian. Feel it harden around you.

Envision the obsidian absorbing into your every pore, slowly transforming you into the very same obsidian, until you are one with the obsidian sphere, no longer a body. Hold your breath and imagine what it would be like to be forever petrified within that lava rock. Imagine not even having the opportunity to suffocate, for the obsidian filled your insides and airways too quickly.

Breathe. Now, envision the Aegishjalmur slowly reappearing with every inhale, just the helm inside the sphere, like revived lava. Watch, as this lava Helm spreads to reform your body within the sphere. Now, you are as a lava being inside the obsidian sphere.

Keep your eyes closed and stand. Flex every muscle in your entire body and recite this passage in the loudest, most intimidating voice that you can manage.

Black fire! Red Fire!
Savior and Destroyer,
I am power!
Tremble before me!
Behold! I am Lokessen!

Open your eyes and scream in the loudest, most intimidating voice that you can manage. Release your flex and, in doing so, envision the obsidian sphere exploding and shattering around you.

***

You have completed your ritual. But the journey doesn't conclude here. You've only fortified your Cosmic Energy field. This will keep your energy within your field from being externally absorbed by others or any external source. However, the ritual also keeps you from absorbing energy from external sources. Therefore, there is a secondary ritual to only be performed when you are completely certain that the energy is what you desire.

There are certain stones that carry with them specific vibrations that can amplify your intentions in the same manner as that of talismans, charms, sigils, the round towers of Ireland and their Schumann waves, and so on. Each stone has its own attributes for varying purposes. Many prefer to covet large collections to suit their multifaceted needs.

The Satanic Order av Wyrd only appropriates two such stones, labradorite and the standard natural quartz. It is our assessment that these two stones secure all requirements in respect to amplification demands. It's not a requirement, using these stones, merely an option.

Labradorite

The labradorite stone's properties link us to the spirit world, a dimension where anything is possible. Other stones keep us anchored to the earth with their powerful grounding effects while Labradorite extends its reach into the universe. Labradorite inspires you to reach for the stars in your quest for higher consciousness. It bridges the gap between realms, so that your dreams and aspirations are not so out of reach. In this way, a labradorite stone is one of the most powerful stones that can support your intentions by giving you the will to strive for what you truly want without placing any limits on what you can achieve.

Labradorite will seal your aura to prevent any energy leaks. It will help you to boost your abilities and promote energetic growth. It will also sharpen your intuition, allowing for good timing and decision-making in the face of adversity. In addition, the labradorite stone promotes fortunate coincidence and an advantageous flow of synchronicity.

The Natural Quartz

Quartz is the most powerful healing and energy amplifying stone there Isaiah It has a unique helical, spiral crystalline form, which enables it to effortlessly absorb, store, and balance all kinds of energy vibrations. Holding a quartz crystal in your hand doubles your biomagnetic field and this can be verified through the use of a Kirlian camera. The quarts can also tap into the subconscious, enhancing memory and intelligence.

Evidently, one could see why having these stones would support one's cause. We like to think of them as a perk, but maintain the utmost respect for them, while engaging in our daily endeavors. you'd do well not to underestimate their powers.

Loke's Snare

The following ritual is rather simple, in that all you need to do, after careful consideration of why you're doing it, is to whisper two incantations through your teeth, as you clench your teeth and fists as tightly as you can. These incantations, however, are extraordinarily powerful sentences and, again, having your stones with you can amplify your means. Remember: you only want to let the energy in when you are completely certain that the specific energy is what you desire.

The first incantation will be said prior to absorption. The second will follow the absorption. The absorption should take approximately five minutes. Within this time, envision, with every inhale, that the other's energy is flowing into you. If you are skilled in seeing Cosmic Energy and its associated fields, you will surely bear witness to this transpiration.

1.
My sphere is a black hole
and, around us, his snare,
where nothing escapes
and nothing is spared.

2.
Satiated, a champion,
I've arrested my prize,
my sphere and my power
now galvanized.

***

As soon as you've finished the second incantation, your sphere will return to its fortified state. Be calculative in this ritual's regard. With great risk comes great opportunity, but only if you're fully aware of the associated gratuity.

CHAPTER IV

Our Views and Their Practical Applications—Section III—Fear

fear

['fir]

NOUN

1. an unpleasant, often strong, emotion caused by anticipation or awareness of danger.

F ear is an extremely powerful emotion, capable of destruction, not only to the self, but to others, intermittently on a massive scale. Comparatively, one can say that fear is the most effective and powerful emotion or, in a sense, energy in existence. Fear transcends age, in that nearly everyone experiences it, in one form or another or in many forms, on innumerable occasions within their lifetimes. Correspondingly, fear also has the ability to make a presumably mature adult regress to his or her most juvenile, unsophisticated, nearly infantile state.

Example I—The Terroristic Toxic Gas Incident—1995

In 1995, a group of religious terrorists released toxic sarin gas into the Tokyo subway system. As a result, over five thousand people poured into hospitals claiming to be experiencing the symptoms associated with toxic gas exposure, including dizziness and nausea. However, after testing patients, doctors found that more than 70 percent of the people who fell ill were not even exposed to the gas at all, but were subjected to fear-based, mass hysteria.

Example II—The Tennessee High School Toxic Gas Incident of 1998

In 1998, at a high school in Tennessee, a teacher complained of a pungent gaseous aroma in her classroom. Soon after, she became ill, experiencing symptoms of nausea, shortness of breath, dizziness, and a headache. Without hesitation, a great number of students in the classroom started to experience similar symptoms, and not long after, the rest of the school was afflicted.

The school was evacuated, as Firefighters, ambulances, and police arrived on the scene. That night, their local ER had admitted eighty students and nineteen staff members. It was a fucking madhouse.

What was the mysterious toxic gas that provoked such disorder? After several comprehensive investigations, government agencies found nothing. Blood tests showed no signs of any harmful compounds. In fact, according to Timothy Jones, an epidemiologist, the fear of being poisoned was so great and had spread so rapidly that the fear itself and the mind's powerful ability to materialize a myriad of items produced the symptoms experienced by everyone involved. Additionally, the *New England Journal of Medicine* attributed the outbreak to a phenomenon known as *mass psychogenic illness*, which can occur when the fear of infection spreads as quickly and vigorously as the disease itself.

Example III—Strawberries with Sugar Virus of 2006

In May 2006, an outbreak of the so-called Morangos com Açúcar virus (strawberries with sugar virus) was reported in Portuguese schools. The virus was named after the popular teen girl's show, Morangos com Açúcar (Strawberries with Sugar). Three hundred or more students at fourteen schools reported similar symptoms to those experienced by the characters in an episode in which a life-threatening virus infected the school depicted in said show. Symptoms included rashes, difficulty breathing, and dizziness. The belief that there was a medical outbreak forced many schools to temporarily close. The Portuguese National Institute for Medical Emergency eventually dismissed the illness as fear-based, mass hysteria.

***

So what causes fear? Why do we feel this emotion? Is it a weakness or is it a strength? Is it a sign of intelligence or a lack thereof?

According to many professors, scientists, doctors, etc., fear triggers a primitive part of the brain known as the amygdala. When we're afraid, the amygdala becomes highly active, as seen through fMRI scans. The amygdala is an almond shaped structure that resides in a lower portion of the brain, the limbic system, and is thought to have developed early on in our evolutionary history to help us avoid becoming victims or sustenance for a multitude of predatory creatures.

The amygdala's activation coincides with the bodily response associated with fear, such as increased heart rate, blood pressure, sweating, and so on. When it perceives a threat, the amygdala triggers nervous responses and stimulates the production of hormones that affect the body. It's also connected to the hippocampus. This is where we store our memories.

Unfortunately, the forebrain, the most evolved portion of the brain, has difficulty overriding the reactions of the amygdala. This results in irrational fear. But there are solutions.

The amygdala has remained unchanged since our beginnings and certainly serves a purpose, to an extent. However, it can also obstruct physical progress, feats of strength, and, generally, the ability to think on your feet and prevail in the face of adversity. Fortunately, as evolution would have it, we now have the neocortex. Other terms commonly used for it are the rational brain or the higher brain. This is supposed to be the wise brain.

Being wise and strategic about modern world issues requires you to usually pause, reflect, weigh pros and cons, and proceed. These are deliberate actions. They're not automatic and visceral like our emotional impulses of the amygdala. But being wise and strategic in this modern world, strengthening and refining the neocortex, the practice of accessing rationality by slowing down, pausing, reflecting and choosing appropriate action, takes time and effort, practice.

Too often do people end up selecting distortions, both cognitively and behaviorally. This trains your amygdala to raise louder alarms. The louder alarms need more assistance, more distortions, and, eventually, you begin a downward spiral that is extremely difficult to remedy.

If you follow these distorted patterns for too long in your life, from too early in life, or in too many areas of life, the stress response is perpetually active in your body. Soon enough, these are what you'll have to accept as labels for yourself: worrier, neurotic, hyper, type A, crazy, bipolar, anxious, depressed, manic, weak link, lost cause, and the like. This becomes your conditioning, you self-defeating, puny, worthless cunt. Is this what you'd wish upon yourself? Wake the fuck up.

There are those who say that fear is a necessary evil, in that it protects us from blindly wandering into danger. The Satanic Order av Wyrd wholeheartedly disagrees. Fear is not a necessary evil. In fact, fear isn't evil and fear isn't necessary. It's a hindrance and a nuisance, and,if you are to be one of us, a Lokessen of the Satanic Order av Wyrd, you'll do well to free yourself of this burden, and we will help you.

Those who are Lokessens of the Satanic Order av Wyrd and the prime candidates who will become Lokessens in the future are likely to lack fear, even to a worrisome degree, and to those and theirs I say kudos. Keep up the good work. But for those of you who aspire to be brought into the fold and experience fear, if even for moments over an elongated length of time, what you'll need to do is to retrain your amygdala and refine your neocortex.

The following are exercises that will do just that. But remember: this will take time and effort, a regiment, a conditioning that'll reconfigure your mind, body, and Wyrd.

Keep in mind the amygdala can only be trained by changing behaviors and memory replacement. Of course, behavior is guided by thinking. S, what thoughts and philosophies will guide you to behave correctly, to rid yourself of anxiety and stress, or, in other words, fear?

You need to drop the distorted patterns, mentioned previously, but don't force them to disappear from your head. Just knowing that your conditioned thinking has been distorted is the first step, but forcing your brain not to produce old thoughts, thoughts that you've been thinking for so long, is self-defeating and a big mistake, one that you've been making for so long. You cannot manipulate your thoughts. The amygdala and your subconscious won't let you, truly. But you can develop new thinking along-side those distortions. Much like the shunt of the electronic world: Picture Christmas lights. When a filament burns out in one of the incandescent light bulbs, the full line voltage appears across the burnt-out bulb. A shunt resistor, which has been connected in parallel across the filament before it burned out, will then short out to bypass the burnt filament and allow the rest of the string to light. This is what you'll do. You will apply a shunt to your distortions.

First, you need to identify your triggers. Take a week, perhaps two, to really focus on your thought patterns, situations that make you uneasy, subjects that, during conversation, make you feel uncomfortable, and so on. It might help to write down a list of items of which you are consciously aware that cause you fear.

The way to retrain the amygdala is by producing positive memories of yourself when dealing with those triggers. These positive memories cannot be built without action. You need to start somewhere. Where is that? It's with behavior. You need to behave in a way that demonstrates to the amygdala that this conditioned stimulus is not a threat to you.

As stated previously, behavior is guided by thinking. If your old thinking was faulty, don't use it. Use new thinking. But don't force old thoughts to go away. Perceive those thoughts from a distance, from a spectator's point of view, and, instead of traveling that same path, apply your shunt and take the thought into a different direction.

The brain can and does change. Neuroscience has revealed that we can change our brain's wiring at any age. It has been done and it will be done, because neuroplasticity is real.

First off, and I know it sounds rather unoriginal and/or cliché and not at all Satanic, one of the best strategies for improving symptoms of limbic dysfunction is to consume an anti-inflammatory diet. An anti-inflammatory diet eliminates toxic foods that cause inflammation and includes foods that help to reduce inflammation, stabilize blood sugar, and provide necessary nutrients.

Cognitive dysfunction is associated with inflammation, so it is critical to avoid highly inflammatory foods. Highly inflammatory foods include refined sugars and grains, food additives and preservatives, GMO foods, and foods with pesticides and toxic debris. Meat and dairy from conventionally raised animals, farmed fish, processed foods, hydrogenated fats and highly processed vegetable oils, such as canola, grapeseed, and safflower, promote inflammation and should be strictly avoided. These foods and ingredients upregulate inflammation, create extra acidity in the tissues, and poison and destroy brain tissue.

The foods to eat on an anti-inflammatory diet are whole, unprocessed foods. Always choose grass-fed meats, wild-caught fish, and pastured eggs. Include a variety of low-carbohydrate, low-glycemic, colorful vegetables.

Vegetables and fruits have abundant amounts of antioxidants and phyto-nutrients. Antioxidants are compounds naturally found in green vegetables and other foods. They help control oxidative stress in the body and prevent or delay cellular damage. Antioxidants protect your body from chronic disease by neutralizing and removing damaging free radicals from the body, modulating inflammatory processes, and boosting your immune system.

Cruciferous vegetables, leeks, shallots, cucumbers, asparagus, and leafy greens are all good choices for brain health. Low-glycemic fruits include berries, lemons and limes, grapefruit, and Granny Smith apples. Blueberries and lemons are two of the best fruits for brain health. Herbs have powerful anti-inflammatory and brain-healing properties.

Quality fats are a very important part of a brain-healthy diet. Healthy fats are found in coconut, olives, avocados, and their oils and in grass-fed butter and ghee. Omega-3 fatty acids and conjugated linoleic acid (CLA) found in wild-caught salmon and grass-fed beef and dairy are important for brain health.

Omega-3 fatty acids are important for normal brain function. These essential fats improve learning and memory and help to fight against cognitive disorders. Our bodies cannot produce these fatty acids, so we must get omega-3s from dietary and supplement sources. The aforementioned wild-caught, fatty fish like salmon, as well as sardines and walnuts are good sources of omega-3 fatty acids.

I know. By now, I'm sure you're altogether baffled. Cosmic Energy, Satanism, the Norse belief system, Social Darwinism and Racial Hygiene, and a healthy, well-balanced diet, what the fuck is going on here? Well, as I said before, this is to rid yourself of fear and anxiety so that you may move forward within the Satanic community, an unstoppable force and a valuable asset. There is a method to our madness and, if you can make it through this manuscript and ultimately decide to take this journey, when you find success and become a force to be reckoned with, I'll be available, anytime, to receive your praise and thanks!

Stress is one of the leading factors in cognitive dysfunction. Severe stress causes inflammation in the brain. This inflammation, as anyone would assume, has a negative impact on brain health.

The importance of stress management was exemplified by a study that identified twenty-seven stressful life events that can cause permanent damage to the brain. These stressful experiences were found to age the brain by several years. The study found that even events early in life may have an impact on later brain health showing the need to reduce stress throughout your lifespan.

A 2018 study had similar results. The study looked at the impact of negative, fateful life events on the brain. The researchers found that having more stressful events in life was associated with advanced brain aging.

Stimulating activities can help reduce stress and engage the brain. Activities such as playing games, reading books, and art can help reduce cognitive impairment. Listening to music can help minimize stress and may facilitate brain neurogenesis.

Sensitivity to electromagnetic fields (EMFs) can play a role in limbic dysfunction. An EMF is a physical field produced by an electrically charged object. These include cell phones, microwave ovens, WiFi, smart meters, and more.

There are a broad range of symptoms associated with EMF sensitivities. I know that it can be difficult to grasp, both the impending harmful effects and using less of those items that caused said harmful effects. But, if you consider that these symptoms include cognitive issues, insomnia, fatigue, dizziness, joint pain, palpitations, and ringing in ears, you may change your tune. I'm not saying to stay away from them permanently. Any way you can trim usage will help.

Restorative sleep is critical for optimal brain function. Sleep reduces inflammation and restores the brain by flushing out toxins. One of these toxins is a toxic protein called beta-amyloid that accumulates in the brains of patients with Alzheimer's. Sleep also allows the neurological system to upregulate appropriate neurotransmitters and rebuild myelin sheaths that protect and insulate nerve fibers.

A lack of sleep significantly impacts cognitive function, impairing reasoning, problem-solving, attention to detail, and so on. Sleep deficiencies cause blood sugar imbalances, increase inflammation, and increase cortisol secretion, which may contribute to cognitive problems as well.

Magnesium is an important micronutrient that plays a critical role in stress and sleep. Supplementing with magnesium, such as Brain Calm Magnesium, may help the brain signal the body for sleep. Marijuana, within reason, can also help with restful, truly restorative sleep.

Improving neuroplasticity does not have to involve brain games with complex algorithms compiled by a team of neuroscientists. It's not that complicated. Below are examples of a broad range of brain exercises you can fit into your daily life.

Immersing oneself in intellectually stimulating activities provides a brain workout, so to speak. They could include online courses, debates, or board games. Challenge your brain by doing common tasks differently. Rather than hiking your regular trail, if you do this sort of thing, find a new trail to explore. If you do Tibetan Buddhist meditation each week, drop in on a Zen class and bend those brainwaves in a different direction. If you teach psychology, switch a few classes with a colleague and guest lecture on social psychology, or perhaps you have an interest in behavioral economics. You get the idea. Stretch out your intellectual capacity.

Binaural beats have been shown to promote left and right-brain hemispheric convergence. This promotes whole-brain thinking. If you are a creative person, your right brain will be more developed, and you are more likely to have improved hemispheric convergence. Many people fail to fully develop their right brain but instead lean more on left-brain thinking. But with improved hemispheric convergence, you can master your mind and develop one of today's most sought-after skills: creative, out-of-the-box, right-brain thinking and functional, highly developed left-brain thinking simultaneously.

Playing video games can help. Yes, you read that right. Debate over the potential benefits and risks of video games can get pretty contentious. But, if you enjoy gaming, there's some good news. This hobby can have plenty of cognitive benefits, such as motor coordination, visual recognition and spatial navigation, memory and reaction time, reasoning, decision-making, problem-solving skills, resilience, cooperation, and team participation.

Make music. Music has several neural benefits. It can help improve your mood, ability to learn and remember new information, and concentration and focus.

Music therapy also appears to help slow down cognitive decline in older adults. Research from 2017 suggests music, especially when combined with dance, art, gaming, and exercise, helps promote neuroplasticity. It can improve movement and coordination and may help strengthen memory abilities. But it doesn't just help prevent additional cognitive decline. It can also help relieve emotional distress and improve quality of life.

Learning to play music in childhood can help protect against age-related cognitive decline and lead to improved cognitive performance in older adulthood, for one. Musicians often have better audio and visual perception, greater focus and attention, better memory, and better motor coordination.

It's never too late to learn an instrument. Online tutorials can help you get started, especially if you don't want to splurge on lessons. Check your local classified ads for used instruments.

Not very musical? That's fine. Even listening to music more regularly can help increase brain neuroplasticity. So turn on your favorite playlist. It's good for your brain.

Most people recognize that exercise offers a number of physical benefits, stronger muscles, improved fitness and health, better sleep. But physical activity also strengthens your brain. Exercise, aerobic exercise in particular, can lead to improvements in cognitive abilities like learning and memory.

According to a literature review from 2018, exercise also helps improve fine motor coordination and brain connectivity, and can protect against cognitive decline. It also helps promote increased blood flow and cell growth in the brain, which research links to reduced depression symptoms. How about that—a confident, intelligent, fit Satanist. That is one considerable opponent.

Regardless of all these previously mentioned practices, there are more extreme methods. If you've made it this far and feel that this text resonates with you, you may choose to pursue these over the others. The following are practical applications of the methods integrated and reconstructed by SOW to rid yourself of fear or anxiety:

Operant Conditioning

Operant conditioning, also known as instrumental conditioning, is a method of learning that employs punishments and rewards for behavior. In this method, a link is established between a behavior and a consequence (whether positive or negative) for that behavior. For example, when a monkey presses a button when a LED is on, he's rewarded with a banana. When he presses the button when the LED is off, he receives an electric shock. As a result, he learns to press the button when the LED is on and avoids it when the LED is off. Actually, the monkey forms a link between the behavior (press the button when LED lights up) and the consequences (get a banana).

Operant conditioning was first thoroughly studied by an American psychologist Edward Lee Thorndike in the late-nineteenth century. He advanced a psychological principle called the "law of effect." This law states that actions that result in favorable outcomes have a higher probability of being repeated, while those followed by unfavorable outcomes are less likely to be repeated.

Burrhus Frederic Skinner, an American psychologist, behaviorist, author, inventor, and social philosopher, was a professor of psychology at Harvard University from 1958 to 1974. He theorized that an individual's actions and the consequences of these actions could be used to understand learning and human behavior. He coined the term *operant conditioning.*

Operant conditioning is a modified version of the law of effect and relies on an equally simple premise. Actions followed by reinforcement will be strengthened and are more likely to be repeated in the future. Similarly, actions that are followed by punishment are weakened and are less likely to be repeated.

Another important consequence is extinction, which occurs when a response that had previously been reinforced/punished is no longer effective. For instance, if you stop rewarding a monkey with a banana every time he presses a button, he will press the button less often and eventually stop. In this case, the button pressing would be said to be extinguished. This concept is often advocated in Pavlovian extinction, a more passive and less direct approach, one with which we won't be engaged.

Many things we do are either directly or indirectly influenced by operant conditioning, such as students being applauded for an oral presentation or for winning a debate, versus being ridiculed, or training a dog to sit, or discount or loyalty programs. However, this concept can be applied on a more radical, self-initiated level. SOW promotes this radical operant conditioning and offers these phases to overcome your fear and anxiety, in order to become all that you can be, as well as a valuable asset to your Satanic organization, the Satanic Order av Wyrd.

The VI Phases of Pain

We spend so much of our time avoiding pain, emotional and physical. But to what end? In fact, the endurance of pain, emotional and physical, makes us stronger and more knowledgeable. That is to say, the more pain we feel, the more detached we become from that pain, and the more aware we are of that pain, the more we know what to expect when we are about to experience it again, thus having less of an effect or shock value on the overall experience. As a result of this inadvertent conditioning, we also fear the source substantially less or not at all. Therefore, it is prudent to maintain that enduring more pain, emotional and physical, is a mechanism, to be used in association with other mechanisms, with which we can rid ourselves of fear. This is our VI Phases of Pain.

The VI Phases of Pain start rather insipid and gradually become more intense. Once you've reached the sixth phase, you should be well on your way to not only generally fearing less, but you'll be viewing life in a different light, as well. Do not, under any circumstances, cut corners or deceive yourself in pursuing these phases. If you do, you'll only be cheating yourself, and when the time comes, when you're placed before SOW for review, we will know what you've done.

In regards to operant conditioning, your reward will not be material. Your reward will be that you've successfully completed The VI Phases of Pain. Your reward will be that you're a fearless, strong individual whose knowledge of the self has matured. Your reward is that you're six steps closer to becoming a Lokessen of the Satanic Order av Wyrd!

Phase I—The Humiliation Declaration

The first phase is quite simple and takes little physical effort to accomplish. You'll need to go somewhere reasonably populated, such as a food court in a mall or a grocery store. However, the recommended venue is a Christian church on Sunday morning, during mass, and you'll want to dress in attire that is easily removable but semiformal, nonetheless.

Enter the cathedral, chapel, mosque, perish, or what have you. Center yourself among the Christians, standing, and begin to remove your clothes. You may wear your undergarments.

Scream in the loudest, most intimidating voice that you can manage. Then cry or simulate crying in a pathetic, desperate, hysterical manner.

While crying, reach out your arms or hands to those closest to you. If there exists a sympathetic person or persons who attempt to take your hands in theirs, slap their hands, while shouting gibberish.

Gather your clothes and slowly vacate the premises. You've completed the first phase. You're ready to move on to the second.

Phase II—The Revealing of Truths

People lie. It's part of being human. Whether they're substantial and incriminating or simple so-called white lies, they're ever present in our lives on a regular basis and we're no exception.

I had the privilege of speaking to three psychologists of private practices who each revealed a story of one of their many clients. The first was a woman, in her late thirties, who struggled with her parents' reaction to her falling in love with a man from another culture. The second revealed that a young man who finished law school, secretly pursued a career in comedy for a decade, before he told his family. Finally, the third revealed that a middle-aged man had told his wife and kids, since the beginning of their relationship and since the children could comprehend such information, that he was a military combat trainer for a great deal of his life, before ultimately changing careers. As a result, they, his family, had spent their lives shrouded in a false sense of security, until one of his teenage children looked into the validity of his claim. Once confronted with too many difficult questions, the man finally came clean. His wife and children were devastated.

The psychologists stated that they encouraged their clients to disclose their secrets, and in the aftermath, they would be forced to summon the courage and discipline to attempt ongoing understanding and healing with family and friends who had negative responses. Whether or not those close to these people accepted or even embraced the changes, however, was less important than that individual making the decision to tell the truth and stand his or her ground. Many of the psychologist's patients, who were given these directives, felt a huge sense of relief after clearing the air, so to speak, because they no longer had to carry the weight of the secret(s). They could just be themselves, fully, without worrying about maintaining a false front.

If your identity is based on the views of others and you rely on those views to maintain your reality, you, in all honesty, don't know yourself at all. You're a weakling and a parasite. You're a disposable entity, trash.

Many psychologists, life coaches, authors, and unsolicited advisers will tell you that this task requires finesse or delicacy, or both, that you should hold out for the opportune moment, that you should reassure the recipient of your truths that you're still the same person, that you should be aware of your feelings and comfort levels and work through your guilt and shame before acting. To SOW, this is bullshit! You deserve this rude awakening. You need this most awkward of situations to inflict pain back at you and you need to endure it. Reap what you SOW.

Consequently, you will gather those who mean the most to you, those to whom you've lied, whether they were little white lies or substantial, possibly incriminating lies. Reveal to each person the lies that you've told them. Reveal the truth behind those lies.

While revealing the lies and the truths behind those lies, keep a straight face. Don't use body language. Don't seek sympathy. Remain neutral, seemingly unscathed by what is unfolding.

Wait for their responses. Listen to each response intently. If your honesty results in breaking these bonds of friendship or family, so be it, for they don't care for you enough to support you through your trials and they can't see your transformation of becoming a stronger, fearless being, as well as a valuable asset to a crucial and robust organization.

As the phase draws to a close and weeds out those who revealed their true colors, in a negative sense, excuse yourself. Find a place where you can be alone and comfortable. Reflect on what has transpired. Congratulations. You've completed phase II.

Phase III—The Pilfering Pick-Me-Up

This phase has versatile significance to SOW. Not only will you encounter more emotional and possible physical pain by addressing a multitude of fears, such as the fear of incarceration, the fear of confrontation, the fear of vulnerability, the fear of being attacked, scopophobia, etc., but you will also experience the semi-involuntary reward of increased serotonin and dopamine levels. In addition, you'll seize yet another opportunity to mock the Christian god, among others, by committing one of the more effective sins, theft, and you'll be paying homage or tribute to, by virtue of the tales of thievery associated, our beloved Satan, Loke.

All that is required of you in this phase is that you stroll into a grocery store or mini-market or retailer of some sort and steal or shoplift a single item. Once you've chosen and seized your item, proceed to the exit and leave. If you are pursued, run. If you are apprehended, so be it.

When you think of retail theft, you might envision teenagers shoplifting candy or headphones or something similar. It's much more than that. People from all walks of life and all ages steal. More than $44 billion in merchandise goes missing across the United States each year.

According to many psychologists and professors, and, specifically, one professor at the University of California, San Francisco, an act of theft can bring forth someone's hidden traits, paradoxically proving beneficial to their personal development. Essentially, this was or is the sole purpose of this phase. Congratulations, you've successfully completed phase III.

Phase IV—The Scales of Skirmish

That which does not kill us makes us stronger."

—Friedrich Nietzsche

As Nietzsche was more cerebral and physically quite fragile, we assume that his quote was directed toward the emotional and cognitive aspects of strength. However, he did suffer from syphilis and was sickly for most of his life. So he could've been referring to the physicality of pain and suffering and the ability to overcome suffering, resulting in the celebration of suffering.

Regardless, this quote, in itself, is the sole inspiration for this phase. But, as per usual, our reasons are multifaceted. Those arguments are as follows:

- Stress and fear, to an extent, are the body's responses to emergencies. They occur naturally when we are exposed to danger or even when we're anticipating danger. We've already discussed the implications therein. But prolonged stress and habitual fears in everyday life have negative impacts on health. Stress and/or fear can manifest as worry, irritability, restlessness, insomnia, anger, dread, and many more mental symptoms. Physically, stress and/or fear can cause muscle tension, headaches, back pain, dry mouth, clammy skin, indigestion, frequent urination, rapid pulse, and breathing problems. With such a long list of symptoms, it's obvious that we need active ways to relieve or treat such ailments. Physical activity can help alleviate stress and fighting for the sake of fighting, in particular, has numerous mental and physical health benefits.

- In addition, fighting for the sake of fighting results in the release of endorphins, the neurotransmitters that elevate your mood. Physical activity also reduces stress hormones such as adrenaline and cortisol. In other words, When you fight, it brings your stress and fear or anxiety levels down on a neurochemical level.

- Fighting also impacts your concentration. When you're fighting, it's easy to forget everything else that's on your mind and just focus on punching or kicking or headbutting or whatever, because it requires all of your attention and moves at a quick pace. As a result, when you're fighting, you can shut out the stressors in your life, allowing you time to better deal with your problems or gain a new perspective on them.

- Fighting, as we all know, has its advantageous byproducts: physical benefits, such as weight loss, strength building, etc. But it has significant mental and emotional benefits as well. In addition to relieving or absolving stress and fear, fighting improves your concentration, helps you manage anger, promotes social growth, and boosts your self-esteem.

Considering the catalogued, there is no reason why we wouldn't implicate this, the fourth phase. But, above all other benefits, our primary causes for this phase are to clear the mind within an instant, provide a new perspective on life, and to exterminate your fears of fighting or the fears of the dangers associated with fighting in the future. Your task is as follows:

You will find a willing friend, acquaintance, or choose a complete stranger to fight you. Whether it is an accord with the other or violently and abruptly provoked, you will fight. If you've never endured a fight, there's a first time for everything. Make sure that the location is somewhat secluded or populated in a manner that a display such as this doesn't negatively impact spectators; and, if you're apprehended by police officers, so be it.

Unfortunately, whether it is your first or your twentieth, you're not going to win this one. By all means, do try. However, for this exercise, we want you to experience the full extent of the ordeal, the exertion, the pain, the defeat, and so on. So if you find yourself approaching victory, throw the fight, and endure. If you find yourself in a situation where you're facing a detrimental, gruesome defeat, by all means, retreat. But you'd better have some battle scars, so to speak.

Afterward, go home. Reflect. You've successfully completed phase IV.

Phase V—The Death Directive

There are two elements of fear associated with death, necrophobia and thanatophobia. Both are very much absurd and unacceptable. If you experience either of these irrational fears on a regular basis or even a semiregular basis, you'll do well to overcome them, and we will point you in the right direction.

A person with necrophobia is incredibly anxious when it comes to death and is afraid of dying themselves as much as they are afraid of dead things, whether they're human or animal. The necrophobic's fear can also be associated with dead things like coffins, graveyards, and the like. In these cases, necrophobia is a fear of the dying, rather than the fear of the actual act of dying.

Because of the high level of fear and increased anxiety that results from necrophobia, other mental health issues can develop like agoraphobia (fear of certain places) and insomnia (trouble falling/staying asleep). These thoughts can become especially traumatic when the death of a close family member occurs. In children, an occurrence like this can compromise the ego's integrity and result in a consistent, elongated psychological condition.

Thanatophobia is a disorder characterized by an extreme fear of dying. Because necrophobia and thanatophobia are similar phobias, many people get the two confused.

Although they are very similar, the two disorders have significant differences. People struggling with thanatophobia may not be afraid of dead bodies, coffins, and can even attend funerals. Their fear isn't centered around the death of others as much as it is the possibility of dying themselves. People with thanatophobia have related symptoms like the fear of flying and also the aging process. There might also be an underlying fear of being buried or cremated after death. In a medical setting, thanatophobia is commonly called *death anxiety*.

It is presumed that the primary basis of these irrational fears is the lack of control over one's own life or the lives of others. But as we've discussed previously, chaos is one of the primary ultimate truths of the universe and cannot be altered. In a sense, this unwarranted sense of entitlement that humanity seems to hold so dear is nothing more than delusion, self-deceit. You're much better off making death a part of your life. That means committing to staring down your death fears, whether it be your death, the death of those you love, the pain of dying, the afterlife or lack thereof, grief, corpses, bodily decomposition, or all of the above. Accepting that death itself is natural and essential is rational and rewarding in so many ways. The fears associated with death and all that death entails, on both personal and cultural levels, are very unnatural and a burden.

You will start this multifaceted phase by preparing for your death. Get your affairs in order. Designate a power of attorney, prepare for your memorial service, have a will in place, and so on.

There are many ways you can rid yourself of these fears, therapy or counseling, focus groups, exercises like focusing on the here and now or exploring spirituality or philosophy. In a sense, you're already doing that. However, the Satanic Order av Wyrd has something a little different in mind.

Now, first, you'll acquire a freshly dead animal, preferably a pig, boar, dog, deer, bigger game, by any means necessary. Get very close to the animal and inhale through your nose, deeply. Smell the cold, the metallic scent of blood, a possible underlying aroma of feces and urine, the scent of meat, the gamey, somewhat sweaty, pungent odor.

Touch the corpse. If there is an open wound, reach in and fondle the innards. If there isn't an open wound, make one.

Move away from the corpse, just a few paces, and stare at the corpse. Imagine the hardships that it faced throughout its life. Contemplate the hardships of the world. Contemplate the emotional trauma you've endured throughout your own life. This animal is free from all of this, no longer a prisoner to the mortal coil and the mortal husk, and, if your necessary means of acquiring this animal was murder, then you set the animal free. Well done.

Now, acquire the series *Faces of Death*, or view Rotten.com or *The Many Faces of Death*, or something similar. Subject yourself to the videos. Watch whatever you've obtained in their entirety. If you feel sick or overwhelmed, keep watching. Muscle through it. You can do thIsaiah

Now, acquire these works: *Tomino's Hell*, *The Orphan's Story*, *The Book of the Sacred Magic of Abramelin The Mage*, *The Lesser Key of Solomon*, and other texts, if possible, that carry the same overall proclamation, that, if you read these texts, you're cursed to die or go mad or be visited by evil entities, or the like. Research them before reading. Read them in full. Go through the motions that reading these books entail. Endure the stages of acceptance and carry on. You've successfully completed phase V.

Phase VI—The Rest Stop Repeat

This phase is a break, a rest stop, a moment to process and unwind after everything you've accomplished thus far. Take a moment to reflect. Once you feel that you've rejuvenated and overcome certain faulty wiring, so to speak, within the brain, repeat phases I–V, once more. You may even consider completing the VI Phases of Pain a third time and, if you sincerely feel that it's necessary, then, by all means, do so. We do not condone a fourth reiteration.

Congratulations! You've successfully completed the VI Phases of Pain. Well done.

***

Many may find our phases radical, morbid, corporal, and absurd. However, in some circles, our phases may be viewed as ineffective and mediocre. Regardless of either, SOW has witnessed their fruitful results and stands by them.

However you choose to overcome your irrational fears (we've certainly provided a full arsenal of useful tools), we wish you absolute success. When you find yourself free of the burden, you'll be, as stated previously, one step closer to becoming a Lokessen of the Satanic Order of Wyrd. Your will be done.

CHAPTER V

The Shadow Self and the Realization of the Alterna Unu

You've adequately improved yourself on multiple levels up to now. You know more about yourself and your foundations, genetically, spiritually, philosophically, psychologically, and so on, and we applaud you for your successes. But what do you know of your Shadow Self and your Alterna Unu?

Pre-reform, you may have already self-inflicted quite a bit of damage, mentally, physically, and energetically. Fortunately, in part, you've made great strides, mending the wounds of your past and present, paving the way for a greater future. However, more often than not, the human propensity is suppression and repression, and if you're unaware of repressed memories and subconsciously suppressed urges or desires, you wouldn't have known that you needed to remedy this sort of complication. In other words, if you're not aware that there is a problem, then, in your mind's eye, there's no problem to fix.

The Shadow Self

Carl Jung, a Swiss psychoanalyst and psychiatrist who researched the human psyche in the early 1900s, was the president of the International Psychoanalytical Association and is known as the founder of Analytical Psychology. Jung's work has had a profound impact on modern psychology with some of his most important research being his exploration of the human psyche. Psyche, meaning the totality of the human mind, conscious and unconscious, everything in between and anything associated, in essence.

Jung pressed the concept that our conscious mind is where the ego exists, and it's made up of the parts of our personalities and identities that we are aware of. According to Jung, people have personas that are an aspect of personality that comes from a desire to please or be accepted by others. Surely, you can relate. If you're reading this manuscript, you likely have a whole myriad of masks to wear.

The trouble with personas, according to Jung, is that they can lead to aspects of one's personality (both good and bad) being unexplored, under-developed, and suppressed. Through this desire to please others, according to our perceptions of what we've subjectively deemed pleasing, we focus on the associated qualities and hide the parts of ourselves that we believe to be negative or distasteful or what have you. Jung referred to this suppressed side of the personality as the Shadow Self, the parts of ourselves that we think society will disapprove of which are pushed away into our unconscious.

So why is suppressing our Shadow Self detrimental to us? Well, if we're successful in suppressing our more questionable character traits, they are still present in our subconsciouses and can manifest themselves in other ways. Avoiding the dark side of your personality is to cause suffering in the grand scheme of your mortality. Ultimately, the more we suppress feelings and negative emotions into the subconscious, the greater the power they have over us and our surroundings. Moreover, they can assert themselves in different ways. This could be through mental health issues (including, but not limited to, dissociative identity disorder, chronic illness, amnesia, anxiety, addiction, low self-esteem, and something that all SOW Lokessens and many religious and spiritual scholars will substantiate as credible, the Alterna Unu [but we'll get to that later in the chapter]).

Suppressing the Shadow Self prevents us from reaching our full potential. Consequently, most of us have been raised on certain morals and ethical values and it can be hard to break away from something that has been worked into the fabric of our existence since the beginning. But it can happen and it will happen, because you're already well on your way to becoming a complete, formidable asset to the cause and to the powers that be. This is only one more obstacle to overcome on your rise to glory. Keep it up. You're doing great.

The Alterna Unu

As Jung declared, if we're successful in suppressing or repressing our more questionable character traits, our urges or desires, and specific memories, in other words, crucial elements that make up our true being, they are still present in our subconscious and can manifest themselves in other ways. As I declared, SOW Lokessens and many religious and spiritual scholars as well as mystics, shamen, dark arts practitioners, and the like will corroborate that one of the most common ways of this manifestation is the Alterna Unu. This is bad, very bad, for nearly everyone. However, it can be a good thing if you meet and bond with your Alterna Unu, and, in doing so, you'll be accomplishing one of the most pivotal tasks, a task that'll be highly regarded by the Lokessen and the entire Satanic Order av Wyrd.

The Alterna Unu is an alter ego, or alternate personality, an energetic entity that is always with you, an extension of the self, and a full-fledged being, if materialized by power of the psyche. It can talk to you. It can hurt you. It can control you. It can be you. It can alter your perception of reality. It can enter your dreams and silence your screams.

At this moment, you'd likely assume that I'm referring to dissociative identity disorder (DID) and, to a certain degree, I am. But it's so much more than that, because virtually everyone experiences the associated symptoms on certain levels and nearly everyone falls into the same habitual behaviors that Jung, SOW, among select others, deem detrimental to the individual human existence. Furthermore, the Alterna Unu, if materialized, exceeds the realm of DID by becoming a developed material entity.

The patriarch, Abraham, believed that everyone has their own unique, personal demon. In a sense, this is the Alterna Unu. Whether it comes from an outside source or is directly spawned by the self is a different matter.

Regardless, we would like you to consider, momentarily, the nearly inconceivable accomplishments that those applicable have done with, more or less, only their minds, as well as the myriad of unexplained phenomena that occur in our universe on a regular basis:

- The accounts retold in the last chapter are evidence of the mind's ability to materialize legitimate symptoms of illness.
- Multiple military and government factions from all over the globe, including the CIA, continue to open initiatives involving psychic or telekinetic abilities for use by intelligence. Millions of pages of declassified documents have unearthed such initiatives, including, but not limited to the Stargate program, the special laboratory for biocommunications phenomena at the University of Leningrad, the Round Table Foundation of Maine, the military-based Detachment G, and so on, and the subjects therein have accomplished and are accomplishing reality changing feats.
- Despite the prevalence of hoax cases, more and more new cases of the scientific enigma, known as stigmata, have continued to surface over the years. Although there are medical explanations, such as purpura and hematidrosis, there is no explanation as to how they'd occur where they occur (i.e. the tortures of the Christ, Jesus).
- The biochemical implications of the placebo effect have baffled scientists for many years. The only certainty, apparently, is that the mind can affect the body's chemistry and the number of extreme, unbelievable cases increases every year.
- Wim Hof, a Dutch adventurer, ran an Arctic marathon at minus 20 degrees Fahrenheit (minus 29 degrees Celsius), while shirtless. He also holds the world record for being immersed in ice for an hour and forty-four minutes and, in 2007, he was able to survive for seventy-two minutes, outdoors, at the North Pole, while wearing nothing but shorts. Hof says that he is able to control his body temperature by using the Tantric practice of Tummo, which is practiced by Yogi monks in Tibet, and involves the practice of focusing on the body's energies turning them into heat.
- In 2008, Chris Hickman, a Florida firefighter, came to the scene of a car crash in which an older model Chevrolet Blazer had flipped and landed on its side, pinning the driver's arm between the vehicle and

the pavement. Hickman then lifted the SUV about twelve inches (thirty centimeters) off the ground, giving the other firefighters the opportunity to rescue the trapped driver. There are several other cases of these astounding feats of strength.

- The recurring cases of déjà vu and intuition are ever present in human history. You've likely experienced both multiple times in your life. The implications are vast and research into human psychology can offer more naturalistic explanations, but, ultimately, the cause and nature of the phenomenon itself remains a mystery.

- Those involved in the unsolved mysteries of the Bermuda Triangle have accomplished feats that go beyond even their own understanding.

- Brooke Greenberg died at the young age of twenty in 2013. But she didn't look like your average twenty-year-old because her body stopped developing at the age of five. Her hair and nails were the only parts of her body that continued to grow over the years. Despite being born premature, doctors remained perplexed as to why she stopped aging. Numerous DNA studies showed no abnormalities in her genes associated with aging and her parents didn't have a history of abnormal development. Scientists continued to refer to her condition as Syndrome X, a metabolic syndrome. Yet her unusual condition remains unexplained by science.

- Those with highly superior autobiographical memories (HSAM), or eidetic memories, are rare but ever present in the world and throughout history. Brain images of people with HSAM, as well as eidetic memory, have shown researchers that some parts of their brain structure are different from people who have a typical memory. But it's not yet known if these brain differences cause HSAM and eidetic memory or if they occur because the person uses areas of the brain associated with memory more than most.

The strides we've made with genetic engineering, the application of digital technology, the virtually endless implications of physics, chemistry, biology, and so on have all shown us that anything is possible. Additionally, what is thought to be impossible inevitably becomes possible, as time goes on. Taking this into consideration, including the bullet points above and everything else addressed in this manuscript, the possibility of something or someone materializing from seemingly nothing or another realm or from ourselves shouldn't be entirely ludicrous.

In fact, hypothetically, one could theoretically attribute such an occurrence to the measurable substance that is the energy produced by our own biomagnetic or Cosmic Energy field or sphere combined with the immeasurable abilities of the mind, resulting in a chemical reaction on an atomic level that cultivates, ultimately, a separate entity from that of the self, an entity with a consciousness. Stranger things have happened. But, to save some credibility, remember, this is only a hypothetical.

Pseudoscience and theoretical ramblings aside, your Alterna Unu is with you and you need to bond with it. The sooner, the better. So without further delay, here are some steps to help you along the way.

Step I: Locating Your Alterna Unu

You first need to be aware of its presence. To make yourself more aware, you need to ask yourself some questions to recognize the seminal conditions that call for your Alterna Unu. If you are already aware, you can move on to the next step. The elementary questions are as follows:

- Do you feel the presence of another entity nearby at all times or a lot of the time?
- Can you pinpoint its location or general vicinity?
- Do your thoughts change course in a way that is foreign or alien to your usual way of thinking when you become aware of the entity?
- Are these thoughts in your voice or a different voice or accent?
- What were you feeling, emotionally, right before the entity arrived?
- What happens to you physically before the arrival?
- How do you normally act right before the arrival?
- Where and when does the arrival happen?
- Does the entity arrive when other people are nearby?

- Are you aware that this is your Alterna Unu?

The second set of questions will apply during or after the arrival of the Alterna Unu:
- Do you see the Alterna Unu, post arrival, or is it just a voice?
- Can the Alterna Unu move inanimate or animate objects?
- How do you feel during its visit?
- How do you feel immediately after the visit?
- Do you experience any bodily sensations after the visit, like trembling?
- How do you react to the arrival and during the visit?
- Is the Alterna Unu's personality violent, perverted, manipulative, hateful, unhinged, or the like?
- Are you in a different place when this visit ends?
- Does your behavior change after this visit?
- Does the visit attract anyone's attention?
- Does the visit help you or make things worse?

It's a lot to take in—we know. Take your time. Observe and report. Take notes, if necessary. Eventually, you'll be able to predict your Alterna Unu's arrival and be more prepared to interact with it.

Step II: Capturing Your Alterna Unu

Capturing your Alterna Unu is a very difficult task in that you have to connect or bond with it during interaction, then mutually merge with it. It sounds rather simplistic on the page or in theory. I assure you it is not.

Unfortunately, many perceive the Alterna Unu as a demon or poltergeist or some external entity whose sole purpose is to harm you emotionally, mentally, and physically. In a sense, this is true, but it's your fault. You forced it into the darkness and abandoned it. You deprived it of any sort of substantial sustenance. You were ashamed of it, and now it's back with a very personal vendetta!

As a matter of fact, we owe our Alterna Unus our deepest respect and love, because without their existence, we could not have survived with our bodies and minds intact. They took the brunt of the fear and pain that was inflicted upon our bodies and minds when we were too weak to defend ourselves. They took the reins when we needed them most, even if we were unaware of what was transpiring while it transpired.

We can capture the Alterna Unu through the following of the II Phases of the Alterna Unu Alliance to become close to an approximation of being a single unit. Unification means growing closer and closer to your Alterna Unu. Obviously, this means that the gap between the two of you will grow ever smaller, until you, ultimately, become a virtual single unit.

We have already reached awareness. This is a great start. You've also uncovered and possibly resolved multiple aspects of the II Phases of the Alterna Unu Alliance via section III of chapter IV, "Fear."

The benefit from this four-phase process, essentially, is knowing and accepting yourself with all your flaws and beauty, the beauty of becoming one with darkness and transforming it to your benefit. No matter who you are, as a human, you have flaws in the eyes of those around you. But who are they? Where do they get off? Their views and opinions and judgements of you hold no substance.

The II Phases of the Alterna Unu Alliance

Phase I—Identify and Ally

Only after asking yourself the elementary questions and acquiring substantial answers with complete certainty will you then obtain your Alterna Unu's Identity. In order to accomplish such a feat, you'll have to increase your abilities to communicate with yourself, internally, as well as trace your energetic or biochemical signature to its extension, the Alterna Unu. These abilities, within SOW, are summed up into a practice that we call Interspatial Comms.

Interspatial Comms are essentially about mitigating the issues associated with being incomplete. We've already addressed those issues in "The Shadow Self" section of this chapter. There are a few things to keep in mind when engaging in Interspatial Comms:

- Make sure that you have these materials available at all times: notepad or an easily accessible laptop, pen or pencil. You'll want to jot down important details of your visits, prealliance, and you'll want to leave yourself crucial notes for future reference.
- Relax: Between you and your Alterna Unu, relaxation allows for the easiest and most effective interactions. Inducing a trance state via meditation or the initial steps of the Aligning with Yggdrasil ritual from chapter II.
- Acceptance of the existence of your Alterna Unu is crucial. You cannot coexist or interact with a being that you don't perceive as being a legitimate being.

Once your Alterna Unu arrives, welcome it. Introduce yourself and ask its name. Treat this meeting and your line of questioning in the same way that you would a blind date, likes and dislikes, favorite color, music, religious beliefs, hobbies, and so on.

During the interaction, when given the opportune moment, take notes on how your Alterna Unu looks or draw a picture. The purpose of this exercise is to be able to recall every detail of how it looks as well as its characteristics, behaviors, traits, and the like. The more you can retain, the stronger the bond, and if you can empathize and sympathize with your Alterna Unu, you're that much closer to a successful Interspatial Comm session, as well as a more effective capture.

Phase II—Capturing Your Alterna Unu

Once you've bonded through Interspatial Comms and are successful in every associated item thus far, you will choose one of the following:

- A memory that was repressed, but recovered during the preceding exercises.

- A memory that was repressed, but recovered at some point between then and now.
- Guilty pleasures that you've suppressed or strive to suppress.
- Dark desires, secrets or urges, etc.

Your choice and its associated emotions, sensory stimulations, joy, hate, sadness, and the like, will be the pinnacle of your bond. You experienced all of these together before and you will experience them again together. Only, this time, you won't have to hold back or hide anything. You can openly talk about it and share how you viewed the affair and how you view it now.

Once you've reached the apex of your bond, lay down on the floor and request that your Alterna Unu lay directly on top of you. Once it does, let the Alterna Unu absorb into you, slowly vanishing, as the void within is filled. Take the time to let your Alterna Unu settle into you. Feel your strength and confidence increase.

***

Now you've not only gained a powerful ally within and pulled yourself together, but you've strengthened your Cosmic Energy field by a very substantial percentage and your endeavors in the future will be much more effortless. Just remember: from now on, do not suppress urges or desires in the same manner as before. Welcome them and follow through when the time is right.

You'll be surprised to learn that being honest about your intentions in certain circles can be quite rewarding, even if they are dark or disturbing. If the time is right and the conditions are ideal, even darker desires may be fulfilled. You are one with your Alterna Unu. You have control over your Orlog and Wyrd. You fear virtually nothing. You're calculative, progressive, and so on, and you have the power to make your dreams and aspirations a reality.

You've successfully completed the steps and phases contained within this chapter. Do with it what you will. This realm is yours.

CHAPTER VI

Political Views within the Satanic Order av Wyrd

The Satanic Order av Wyrd has, as is increasingly prevalent in our Order (regarding virtually everything in addition to), a considerably unusual approach to politics. In summation, concerning the accusations that we are a national socialist or an anarcho-communist movement, they're only marginally correct. We are, in fact, definitively anarcho-syncretic communists who strive toward the ultimate objective of stateless, or true, communism. But before we dive into that semiunorthodox political title, let's break down the term *politics*.

politics
[pä-luh-tiks]
NOUNNoun
1. A. the art and science of government
    B. the art or science concerned with guiding or influencing governmental policy
    C. the art or science concerned with winning and holding control over a government

Why Politics?

Unwrap the definition to find everything that people do via defining, organizing, and regulating society through campaigns, elections, by making laws, spending, taxing, controlling behavior and managing the economy. David Easton, a bigwig in political science, defined politics as "the authoritative allocation of value." *Authoritative, allocation,* and *value* are the key words in politics.

Things may not always go according to plan. However, someone with *authority* will be able to guide you in the right direction and, ultimately, toward success, for a fee. That authority figure will also divide the spoils ofa said success and distribute the portions as he or she sees fit. This is the *allocation* section of politics. *Value* falls in line with that which we desire: food, shelter, and money, which means retirement programs, health care assistance, support for businesses, public facilities, such as colleges, airports, stadiums, theatres, and public space, such as national parks and forests. Put these three powerful words together and we have politics. It's how we make these kinds of decisions, regarding who gets what and who pays for it.

An ordinary person feels that he or she is too busy in life, working a full-time position, going to school, taking care of family, and so on. They don't have time for city council, state legislature, or Congress. Unfortunately, with this mentality, which is very common in the United States, you forgo the knowledge of how it all works or who's in power and so on and so forth. Then you become oblivious to the massive machine that is your government and you, as an oblivious member of society, are now a malfunctioning component or a burnt-out fuse. But that's not the worst part, if your government starts to falter or heads in a direction that completely goes against everything you think you stand for, you'll have no idea. Forget about being prepared for the inevitable resulting disaster(s) or the negative, personally detrimental, governmental change(s) to come.

We have news for you, you're involved in politics, whether you like it or not, and, even if you think you're coasting by unscathed, think again. Unless you're a bum, living under a bridge, wasting away, you're involved. Politics decides if we go to war and if you'll be sent overseas to fight that war. They decide how we're taxed, what programs get funded, how much tuition will be, which drugs are legal or illegal, what foods are safe or harmful and who is qualified to make these decisions, regarding any of these examples, and so on.

The Three Versions of Politics

1. In this political version, everyone governs themselves. This school of thought argues that the actions of people create the conditions of government. In other words, over a certain period of time the collective people eventually transform into a self-aware, self-sustainable single entity. Aristotle fell into this category. Many consider this to be that of a democratic tradition, because, in this tradition, everyone is expected to participate in order for the system to function properly.
2. In this political version, some people have the knowledge and ability to govern and some people have to be taught. The people who rule themselves without proper instruction will go astray. Plato and Marx fell into this category. Many consider this to be that of an authoritarian tradition, because, in this tradition, if people do participate, more problems will arise than be solved.
3. In this political version, the government is the problem, not the solution, and the institutions of government lead the people astray. Rousseau, Proudhon, and modern anarchists fall into this category. Many consider this to be that of an anarchic tradition, because, in this tradition, it is institutions, not people, who cause the most trouble in the world.

Liberalism, Conservatism, and Capitalism

Obviously, the previous three versions of politics may overlap or fuse, creating many subgenres. Furthermore, none of these are a perfected science and, when you have multiple factions working together to govern an entire country, things can get pretty hairy, as you're probably already aware. Just look at the Republicans and the Democrats of the United States of America.

Throughout history, Athens as well as other states failed as a direct result of multiple political factions attempting to work together to govern. The reason is rather undeniable: the factions, individually, tend to become so obsessed with their own concerns that they forget about everything else. That means that important issues outside their realm of concern are neglected and good leaders are thrown from office over differences regarding associated topics.

Regardless of there being an obvious issue with multiple factions making up our nation's governmental system, it is currently the favored majority vote and, therefore, a state with which we must coexist. These factions are as follows: liberals, conservatives, and capitalists. However, you'll find that the line between capitalists and the other two is quite blurry.

Liberalism in the United States is not quite liberalism in the classical sense of the word. Initially, it was a political philosophy that indicated that the government had a positive position to fill in society. This movement grew as a result of excesses of late-nineteenth- and early-twentieth-century capitalism: No protection for workers, such as a full-time work week with mandatory overtime, child workers chained to factory floors, and very few health, safety, and environmental regulations, protocols, procedures, and so on.

American liberalism began to flourish after the Great Depression. Private charity was completely overwhelmed by the high level of unemployment. So American politics turned heavily toward economics and eventually personal affairs. Liberals fought for more protection for workers and unions, an extensive social safety network for the poor and unemployed, and health, safety, and environmental laws. This approach has its ups and downs: fewer people starved to death, but taxes and costs for businesses and consumers were higher, perpetuated by common consensus through the compliance of more regulations.

Conservatism in the United States tends to call for less government involvement in the economy, a faction that also flourished after the Great Depression. However, they argued that taxes and regulations were actually hampering economic growth and lowering people's standards of living.

Conservatives feel that people should be able to make their own choices about where to spend their money. They favor lower taxes, a balanced federal budget and less regulation of economic systems.

However, Christian conservatives may yield different views that conflict with the ideal order that is the separation of church and state. The Satanic Order av Wyrd does not condone the behavior of Christian Conservatives. Active Lokessens will act toward such an opposition in a myriad of ways that will not be discussed in this literature. If you wish to acquire more information regarding our proactive approaches to Christian conservatives, you will need to become an adept Lokessen.

Capitalism is an economic system based on the private ownership of the means of production and their operation for profit. Central characteristics of capitalism include capital accumulation, competitive markets, price systems, private property, the recognition of property rights, voluntary exchange, and wage labor. In a capitalist market economy, decision-making and investments are determined by owners of wealth, property, or production ability in capital and financial markets, whereas prices and the distribution of goods and services are mainly determined by competition in goods and services markets.

Unfortunately, Capitalism brings power to the hands of a minority capitalist class that exists through the exploitation of the majority working class and their labor. It also prioritizes profit over social good, natural resources, and the environment. Capitalism perpetuates inequality, corruption, and economic instability. Some might say that, if they have the means to topple the competition, so be it, and the economy will benefit as well as the job availability and the like. However, overwhelming inflation of cost for anything they're selling, thus creating monopolies. Governments have passed legislation to keep this from happening. But it happens regardless. Just look at Microsoft, fuel and telecommunication companies, public services, Bayer and Monsanto, Google, Coca-Cola, Pepsi, Johnson & Johnson, Luxottica and Essilor, Kellogg's, Apple, Walmart, Vanderbilt, Intel, and so on. As the economist Branco Milanovic wrote, regarding capitalism, "the entire globe now operates according to the same economic principles, production organized for profit using legally free wage labor and mostly privately owned capital, with decentralized coordination."

As far as liberals and conservatives are concerned, they both have their claws in the capitalist pie, so to speak. Although the percentages point toward conservatives taking a bigger piece of the pie, the liberals aren't far behind them. More and more people are coming around to the realization that this isn't the best way to conduct business when you look at everything from a distance with a wider lens. Even the government and its leadership are realizing the problem.

The mutual absurdity of Trump and Boris Johnson suggests that things are going to get much worse before there is much of a chance that they will get better. It's as Richard V. Reeves said in 2019, "Politically, the challenge is to reassert the authority of government over the market, not in order to cramp competition but in order to see it flourish. The corruption of the government by powerful businesses is not a weird anomaly. It is precisely where market incentives lead. The currency of the political economy is not money, but power." Capitalism works best when it works as a central core that disperses power evenly. It barely works and often doesn't when it focuses that power in choice points of interest. Of course, this concept is widely viewed as a communist or socialist ideology.

Syncretism

The solution, as we can now see as a result of trial and error involving the seemingly endless battle between opposing factions, is political syncretism. Political syncretism, akin to the majority of what the Satanic Order av Wyrd stands for, is the combining of different political beliefs, while blending practices of various schools of thought. In other words, Political Syncretism involves the merging or assimilation of several, successful and rational, varying traditions or specific practices and solutions from multiple factions, thus asserting an underlying unity and allowing for an inclusive approach to politics en masse.

It's not only the most rational choice in politics, but according to SOW, it's the only option. Widening the grasp of power and the ability to blend, evolve, and transform, are essential laws of our hallowed Satan, Loke.

Without syncretism, our political prowess would be limited to single factions, and we won't abide such absurdity.

Of course, our political standpoint isn't complete without chaos, or, at the very least, polarity, even within our own organization. Otherwise, we wouldn't be able to demonstrate diversity in a complete sense. Even within the widened scope of Syncretism, Political Syncretism alone is still regulated by the laws of politics. We needed an X factor, a wild card in our deck (as if we didn't have enough of those already), an ace in the hole: anarchy, or was it syncretism that we needed to add to our anarchism? Well, that's neither here nor there.

Anarchy

When political syncretism isn't enough and the path on which to travel becomes too blurry or vanishes abruptly, where there is no rational vote, because the process has become nothing more than an attempt to refine something hopelessly broken, anarchy is the way. Anarchy has multiple definitions and is subject to change depending on the treatise or publication. However, in the Satanic Order av Wyrd, anarchy is a society or group of people that completely reject a coercive or established hierarchy in situations where there is an absence of any rational or ideal government.

The Satanic Order av Wyrd will take necessary steps to exercise anarchy in an early-twentieth-century form of approach. This means strikes, militancy, unlawful violence and intimidation tactics, and so on, if necessary. We've operated in this manner, on minor and major scales, in the past, and we'll do so again, if politics/government or any substantial, offensive entity gives us just cause.

In these cases of anarchy, our aim is predominantly, *but not limited to,* an alternate system, one based on the abolition of all coercive hierarchy involving the political/governmental state, and advocate for the creation of a system of direct democracy and worker cooperatives. Power to the people! Of course, we're talking about stateless communism.

Stateless Communism

Many would feel that stateless living is primitive. Nothing could be further from the truth. The fact of the matter is that self-sufficient living is what we all strive for, in the grand scheme of things, and self-sufficient living carries with it the ultimate goal of self-sustainability. If done correctly, a self-sufficient society, community, or commune, can be self-sustainable. Unfortunately, most societies convert or subscribe to other forms of government, whereas members of the state reap the majority of the benefits and the people are forced to compete constantly to survive or live comfortably (i.e., democracy, republicanism, most subgenres of communism, and so on).

Many Anarchists, SOW included, believe that communism should be achieved solely through revolution and that the initiatory stage of socialism should be bypassed. This is because authority corrupts its holder and debases its victim, and that a state will never give up power anr wither away voluntarily. We have not achieved this revolution. Let it be known, that true communism, or stateless communism, is a socioeconomic system that has not yet been achieved, as everyone claiming to be communist or socialist have not yet achieved the ultimate goal of self-sustainability, the stateless, classless, moneyless society without government, which we refer as utopia.

However, the Satanic Order av Wyrd does achieve many of the elements of stateless communism on a smaller scale and we do strive to achieve this system on a national scale in the future, hopefully sooner than later. You can do the same by practicing and adopting specific measures associated with communism, such as standing up for what you believe, acquiring land and going off the grid or working to make said land self-sufficient, gardening, hunting, learning numerous trades like blacksmithing, gunsmithing, ammunition smithing, woodworking, carpentry, plumbing, architecture, city planning, welding, elecritionry, explosives tech, anything in the medical field, and so on. The Satanic Order av Wyrd definitely finds these trades, among many others, to be extremely valuable for the cause.

In conclusion, obviously, the ideal state of mind is syncretism, the ultimate goal, stateless communism, by way of early-twentieth-century anarchy, if necessary. These are the political views of the Satanic Order av Wyrd. Did you really expect anything less?

CHAPTER VII

Additional Rituals and Their Objectives

W hy Black Magick? Why Ceremonial Magick? Why the rituals and the so-called pageantry?

Black Magick or Ceremonial Magick and the rituals therein predate history. It's one of the oldest traditions that we can know and practice, and there's something to be said for that and its ability to withstand the test of time. In knowing and practicing these, you're undergoing a rite of passage, as well as an artistic/pseudoscientific/alchemical/phenomenal way of life that transcends the boundaries of standard human existence.

Not only does Black Magick play a role in the SOW "foundation" philosophy and not only is it an antiquated, immortal, coveted skill-set practiced by kings, emperors, czars, kaisers, and so on, and many of the world's elite (including celebrities, presidents, vice presidents, members of congress, the global corporatocracy, etc.), as well as great organizations like the Hermetic Order of the Golden Dawn, the Ordo Templi Orientis, the Rosicrucians, the Thule Society, the Fraternitas Saturni, and the like, it's also one of the most effective methods used to manipulate Cosmic Energy, as well as one of the most effective tools for fruition of the implications associated with *mind over matter*. It is an honor to be adorned with such a remarkable legacy. Respectively, I thank the universe for its offering.

The following rituals are only a fraction of the practices contained within the Satanic Order av Wyrd. Understand that, to have full access to our power, you must be an initiated, Adept Lokessen of the Satanic Order av Wyrd. This is the will of the Grandmaster, myself, Imp K. Lokessen.

The Black Mass

The Black Mass is a ceremonial ritual with three objectives. First, it is a positive inversion of the mass performed by the Nazarene or Catholic church and, as a result of the inversion, can also be considered Black Magick. Second, it is a means of personal liberation from general Christian dogma. Third, it is a magickal rite in itself, generating magickal energy that can be manipulated at will.

Many believe the Black Mass to simply be a mockery. This is a common misconception. On the contrary, the Black Mass is a process that takes the energy produced by the Nazarene masses and distorts or perverts that energy for, as stated moments ago, manipulation at will. This is true Black Magick.

Participants often use a consecrated Eucharistic host and desecrate it, using it in obscene ways. This is one of the reasons why tabernacles in Catholic churches have locks and why some parishes have an usher stand next to a communion line. Both policies aim at protecting the Eucharist from being used in the Black Mass.

Interestingly enough, many Satanists are said to know the difference between a consecrated host and an unconsecrated host, being able to sense the presence of God in a consecrated host. For example, if a thousand hosts were put on a table, the Satanist would be able to find the one that was consecrated. This is a sense said to be found in Demons.

A Black Mass will often include priestly vestments and the recitation of Latin prayers, altering the Latin to be focused on Satan instead of God. We take it a step further and use old Norse, in most cases, to further exemplify the perversion of the traditional Christian mass and to stay true to our one true lord, the Satan, Loke. Other rituals included in a Black Mass are sexual in nature and include various perverse sexual acts. It's a celebration of the many sins of man and animal alike and an offense to the Christian God and the Christians equally.

The goal of a Black Mass is the exact opposite of a Catholic Mass. Jesus instituted the Eucharistic celebration to strengthen our communion with God and other people, while the satanic mass sows division and confusion. It's chaos. It's the way of the one true Satan, Loke.

Participants

- Priest—in black robes
- Altar Priestess—in white robes and lay upon the altar naked
- Mistress of Earth—in scarlet robes
- Master—in black robes with Vegvisir painted in blood on forehead and crimson Eihwaz pinned or patched on robe
- Congregation—in black robes

Prepping the Temple

Acquire Frankincense oil to be burned (if possible, accompanied by civet oil), several authentic drinking horns to be filled with strong mead, black candles, several silver patens containing the consecrated cakes (honey, spring water, sea salt, wheat flour, eggs, animal fat) to be previously baked by the Priestess and blessed by the Mistress of Earth.

The Ceremony

The priest signifies the beginning of the Black Mass by clapping his hands together twice. The Mistress of Earth turns to the congregation and makes the sign of the inverted pentagram.

Mistress of Earth: I will go to the altars of Hell.

Priest: To the Satan, Loke, the taker of lives.

All: Our Father which wert in *Ásgarðr*, hallowed be thy name, in *Ásgarðar* as it is in Miðgarður. Give us this day our ecstacy and deliver us to evil, as well as temptation. For we are your kingdom for aeons, until Ragnarøkkr.

Master: May the Satan, Loke, the all-powerful Jarl of Darkness and Lord in the Earth, grant us our desires.

All: Jarl of Darkness, hear us! I believe in one Jarl, the Satan, Loke, who makes the Earth tremble. I believe in one law that triumphs over all, Chaos. I believe in one temple, our temple to the Satan, Loke. I believe in one Word which triumphs over all: the word of ecstacy. I believe in the laws of Wyrd, and, through Orlog, and sacrifice, and the letting of blood, for which I shed no tears since I give praise to my Jarl, the fire-giver, we crave his reign of terror and the pleasures and pain to come, as we've arranged to join you, Satan Loke, in Ragnarøkkr.

The Mistress of Earth kisses the Master, then turns to the Congregation.

Mistress of Earth: May the Satan Loke be with you.

Master: Koma, allr ríkr djǫfull, Loke!

Mistress of Earth: By the word of the Jarl of Darkness. I give praise to you.

The Mistress of Earth kisses the lips of the Altar Priestess.

Mistress of Earth: My Prince, bringer of enlightenment. I greet you, you who causes us to struggle and seek the forbidden thoughts.

Master: Koma, allr ríkr Satan, Loke!

Mistress of Earth: Blessed are the strong, for they shall inherit the Earth.

The Mistress of Earth kisses the chest of the Altar Priestess.

Mistress of Earth: Blessed are the proud, for they shall breed gods!

The Mistress of Earth kisses the vagina of the Altar Priestess.

Mistress of Earth: Let the humble and the meek die in their misery!

The Mistress of Earth kisses the Master who passes the kiss on to the Altar Priestess. The Altar Priestess kisses the lips of each member of the Congregation. Afterward, she hands the paten containing the consecrated "hosts" to the Mistress of Earth and finds her place again upon the altar. The Mistress of Earth holds the paten over the Altar Priestess.

Mistress of Earth: Praised are you, my Jarl and lover, by the strong. Through our evil we have this dirt, by our boldness and strength, it will become for us a joy in this life.

All: Hail the Satan, Loke, Prince of Life!

The Mistress of Earth places the paten on the body of the Altar Priestess.

Mistress of Earth: Taka, Loke, gumi kostr muna Loke sem villieldr.

Priest: Andi líkami Loke.

The Priest, while quietly saying this, begins to stimulate the Altar Priestess's genitals with the fingers of his left hand, while stimulating his own with his right hand. As he does, the Congregation begins to clap their hands and shout in encouragement.

Master and Mistress of Earth: Koma, allr ríkr Satan, Loke!

The priest ejaculates on the "hosts'"hosts' and hands the paten to the Mistress of Earth. She holds it up before the Congregation.

Mistress of Earth: May the gifts of our Satan, Loke, be forever with you.

All: As they are with you!

The Mistress of Earth returns the paten to the Altar Priestess and takes up her drinking horn.

Mistress of Earth: Praised are you, my Jarl, by the defiant, and through our malevolence and pride, we have this drink: Let it become for us an elixir of life.

The Mistress of Earth sprinkles some mead over the Altar Priestess and toward the Congregation, then returns her horn to the Altar.

Mistress of Earth: With pride in my heart, I give praise to those who drove the nails and he who thrust the spear into the body of Yeshua, the imposter. May his followers rot in their rejection and filth!

Master: Do you renounce Yeshua, the great imposter, and all his works?

All: We do renounce the Nazarene Yeshua, the great imposter, and all his works!

Master: Do you affirm the Satan, Loke?

All: We do affirm the Satan, Loke!

The Master begins to vibrate.

Master: Várr *áss* Satan, Loke.

The Mistress of Earth picks up the paten with the "hosts""hosts' and turns to the Congregation.

Mistress of Earth: I who am the joys and pleasures of life after which strong men have forever sought, am come to show you my body and my blood.

The Mistress of Earth hands the paten to the Priest who will then take the "hosts""hosts' to the Congregation. They will eat the cakes and drink from their horns. When all have finished, the paten is returned to the Mistress of Earth. She holds it up.

Mistress of Earth: Behold, the dirt of Earth which the humble will eat!

The Congregation laughs while the Mistress of Earth throws the "hosts""hosts' at them. The Congregation tramples the cakes under their feet while the Master continues with his last mantra/vibration. The Mistress of Earth claps her hands thrice to signal to the Congregation.

Mistress of Earth: Dance, I command you!

The Congregation begins to dance counter-sunwise.

Congregation: Satan! Satan!

The Priest catches each member of the Congregation one by one, kisses the lips of each, and removes their robes, after which they return to the dance. The Mistress of Earth stands in the center of the dancers and lifts her hands to the sky.

Mistress of Earth: Let the church of the imposter, Yeshua, crumble into dust! Let all the scum who worship the rotting fish suffer and die in their misery and rejection! We trample on them and spit of their sin! Let there be ecstacy and darkness! Let there be chaos and laughter! Let there be sacrifice and strife! But, most of all, let us enjoy the gifts of death and life!

The Mistress of Earth signals to the Priest who stops the dancer of his choice. The Congregation then pairs off and the orgy of lust begins. The Mistress of Earth helps the Altar Priestess down from the altar and she joins in the festivities. If the Master and Mistress of Earth choose, the energy of the ritual may be used to their will alone.

***

As is the case for all ceremonial rituals, it is helpful if all participants memorize the content and spoken text. Rehearsing allows us to better understand the intention and fine tune the power of the ritual. It is important that these things are done and that the ritual, when undertaken, follows the text on every occasion.

The Death Ritual

Death rituals are abundant all over the world, in many facets, and have been prevalent in culture since prehistoric times. From New Orleans and its jazz funeral, South Korea and its burial beads, to the sky burial ritual in both Mongolia and Tibet, even the Balinese cremation ceremonies, these rituals and ceremonies are often associated with religion as communities follow the traditionally prescribed movements in the wake of a loss of life.

The American public does not deal well with death, although we're very violent in multiple ways, watch movies of murder and mayhem, and read mystery, crime, and thriller books by the truckload. When it comes into our own backyards, however, in many cases, we seem to be at a loss as to what to do. Some have ancestral altars or shrines where they honor and mourn deceased friends and relatives regularly. Some go to therapy. Some commit suicide.

The Satanic Order av Wyrd does not view the deaths of friends or family as something to mourn or agonize over. They're free of the mortal, material realm of existence. This is a good thing.

You'll want to be outdoors for this ceremony, in an isolated location. A funeral pyre is prepared by the Guardian. An ellipse of nine stones should enclose the pyre. Everyone attending should have wooden goblets, to be filled with a strong mead and kept at the ready upon a wooden table of oak away from the pyre.

Participants (all will wear black robes)

- Master
- Mistress of Earth
- Priest
- Priestess
- Congregation
- Guardian

Note: Additional Guardians may be appointed to facilitate access and ensure privacy.

The Ceremony

The body of the deceased member is brought in a light wooden casket, carried by Lokessens of the Satanic Order av Wyrd toward the stones and pyre. It is covered with a crimson drape. After the casket has been placed on the pyre, everyone will gather round, just outside the stones.

Master: Várr *áss* Satan, Loke! We gather here to pay homage to our brother/sister who, by his/her life and magick, did deeds of glory to the honor of our name! Várr *áss* Satan, Loke!

Congregation: Várr *áss* Satan, Loke!

Master: Várr *áss* Baphomet!

Congregation: Várr *áss* Baphomet!

Master: Várr *áss* Jǫrmungandr!

Congregation: Várr *áss* Jǫrmungandr!

Master: Várr *áss* Imp King!

Congregation: Várr *áss* Imp King!

Mistress of Earth: So shall we revering remember the glorious deeds still waiting to be done!

Master: So shall we revering remember the glorious deeds still waiting to be done!

Congregation: So shall we revering remember the glorious deeds still waiting to be done!

The Priest and Priestess hand out the wooden goblets. When this is done, the Master raises his head toward the pyre.

Master: Til Satan, Loke, hverr *ástir* várr *æska*.

The Mistress of Earth then lights the pyre. As it burns, the Master drinks from his goblet, then throws the empty vessel into the flames. The Congregation will then raise their goblets.

Congregation: Til Satan, Loke, hverr *ástir* várr *æska*.

The Congregation drinks and throws the emptied vessels into the flames. The Mistress of Earth is the last to drink. She then throws her goblet into the flames.

Mistress of Earth: May our memories linger to haunt the spaces and the dark! So it has been, so it is, and so shall it be again!

The gathering will then depart from the site. It is the duty of the Guardians to attend to and watch over the pyre, ensuring the casket and contents are reduced completely by the flames. The ashes are to be scattered according to the will of the deceased.

The Satanic Blessing

The Satanic Blessing for The the Satanic Order av Wyrd is used in a myriad of situations whereas the consecrated one is significant to the one who bestows the blessing. Blessing for the sake of blessing is forbidden, as you are, in all actuality, sacrificing a portion of your Cosmic Energy and sacrificing the energies of the universe to benefit your blessed one. You'll do well to make sure that whoever you're blessing is well worth it, now that you're making yourself weaker and asking the powers that be to devote a portion of it, his, her, them, self or selves.

Vibrate the following words toward the person or area you wish to bless.

**Setja _____! Nýta ykkar ríki eða nýta elska
eða orka til mega slá sjá vápn nógu!**

Afterward, with your left hand, extending the forefinger, construct in the air an inverted pentagram, beginning with the bottom right corner in an unbroken movement. When the inverted pentagram is complete, strike the area of your heart on your chest and, if you're blessing a person, strike the area of their heart on their chest as well as you say these words.

Útlægur **ein!**

You have now completed your blessing.

Sigils and Talismans

The Sigil, derived from the Latin sigillum, meaning seal, is a type of symbol used in Magick. The term refers to a type of pictorial representation or signature of a deity or spirit. In modern usage, especially in the context of Chaos Magick, Sigils refer to symbolic representations of the practitioner's will.

In medieval Ceremonial Magick, the term Sigil was commonly used to refer to occult signs which represented various angels and demons in which the practitioner would often summon. The magickal books, called grimoires, usually consisted of pages fraught with Sigils. A particularly well-known set lies within The Lesser Key of Solomon, in which the Sigils of 72 princes of the hierarchy of hell are given for the practitioner's use. Such Sigils were considered to be the equivalent of the true name of the spirit and thus granted the practitioner a measure of control over said beings.

Sigils have a long history in Western Magick. The Golden Dawn evidently familiarized themselves with them, as they combined letters, colors, attributes and their synthesis, to build up a telesmatic image of force. The Sigil then served them for the tracing of a current which called into action a certain elemental force and it was used in the making of Talismans.

Applications of Sigil and Talismanic work were/are ever present in the realm of Runic Magick used by the Germanic peoples and their branches. There will be more on that to come. However, for now, observe meaningful Sigils and Talismans, and their functions, as well as their primary, applicable association to the Satanic Order av Wyrd.

The Primary, Applicable Association to the Satanic Order av Wyrd

Despite the Christiian implications of the Lesser Key of Solomon, among many others, we cherish these books and their practices. The act of advocating the beneficial use of demons, angels, gods, and other spiritual and/or energetic entities alone is enough to merit acceptance by the Satanic Order av Wyrd. Furthermore, as a result of the aforementioned reverent amalgam, we too have the right to access and practice any and all fundamental components of Christianity and/or anti-Christianity. However, we respectfully reject any righteous Christian behaviors or practices, unless merited by natural personal behavior or inverted for the sake of Black Magick for the greater good (applied to personal bias)/evil.

Additionally, it is the belief and demand of the Satanic Order av Wyrd that embracing most religious and/or spiritual practices of most cultures that condone and practice Black Magick or Sorcery, or Witchkraft, or Shamanism, or Cosmic Energetic Manipulation, and so on, are essential to the learning process and, thus, a product of interest, regardless of the belief (s) in the cosmological, theological, philosophical, or scientific aspects involved.

The Lesser Key of Solomon

The Lesser Key of Solomon, also known as Lemegeton Clavicula Salomonis or simply Lemegeton, is an anonymous grimoire on demonology. Compiled in the mid-seventeenth century, it is divided into five books: *Ars Goetia*, *Ars Theurgia-Goetia*, *Ars Paulina*, *Ars Almadel*, and *Ars Notoria*. The materials used for these books are said to be centuries older.

The demons' names encompassing each sigil and ultimately forming the seal are taken from the Ars Goetia, which differ by number and ranking from the Pseudomonarchia Daemonum of Weyer. The purpose of these seals is primarily for the summoning, commanding, or forming an alliance of/ with said demons. The following are the seals and each demon's description, taken directly from the Ars Goetia.

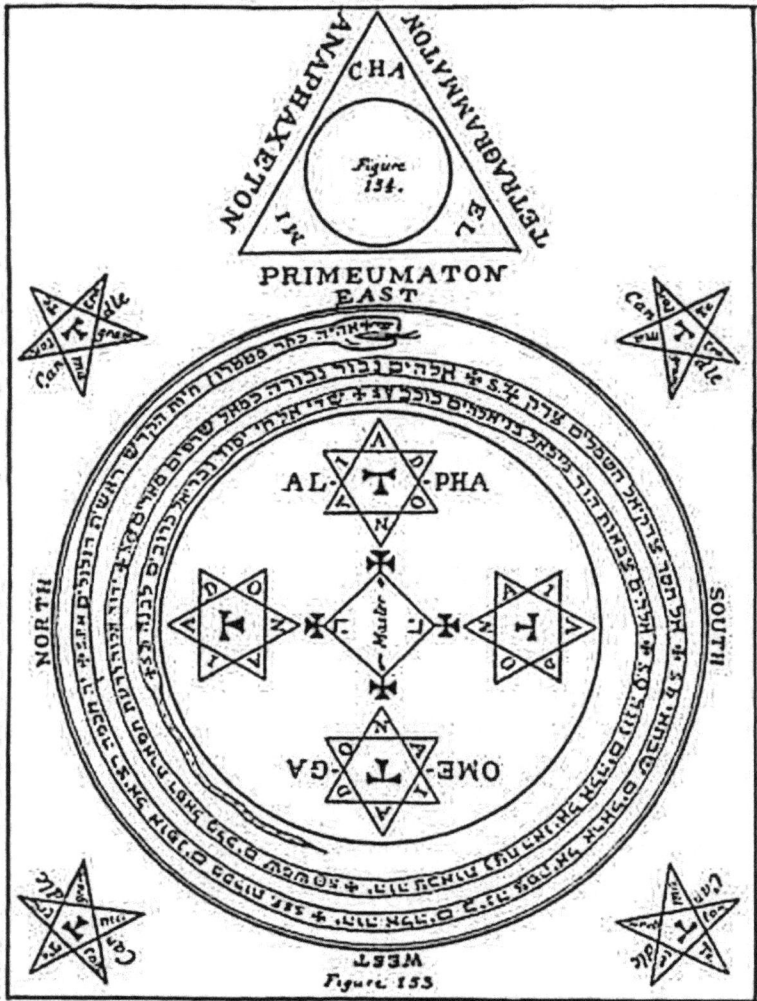

Solomonic Magick Circle with Triangle of Conjuration in the East

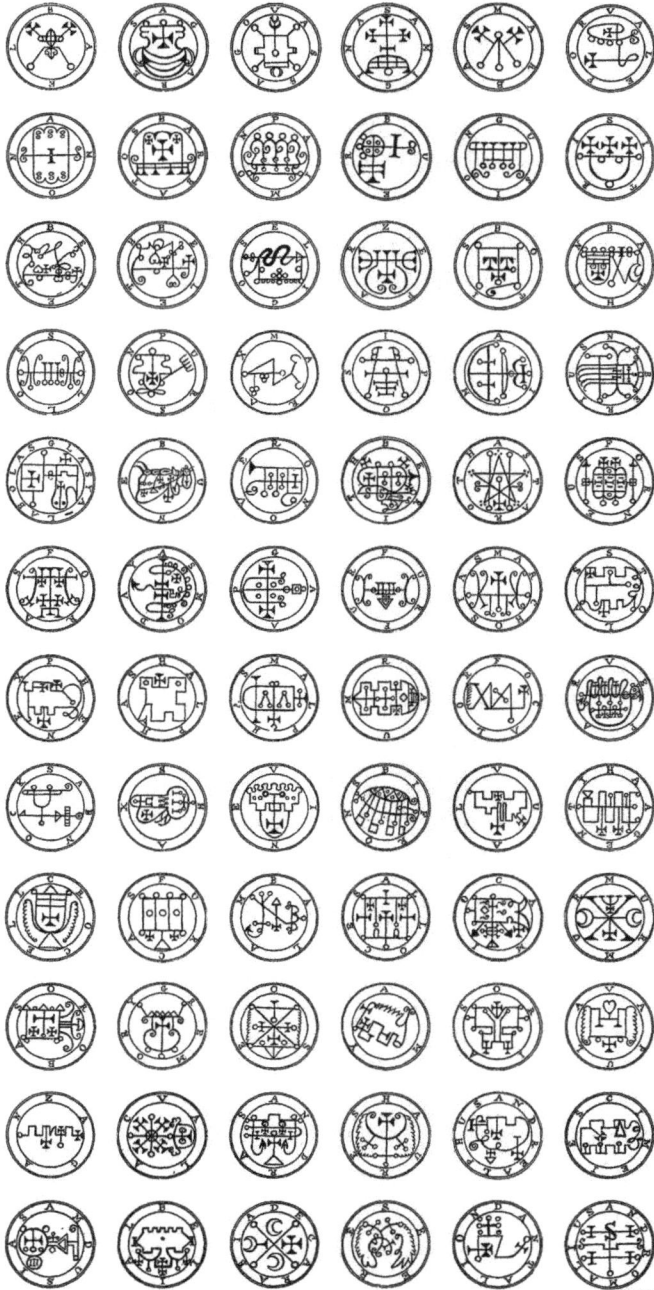

1. BAEL. The First Principal Spirit is a King ruling in the East, called Bael. He maketh thee to go Invisible. He ruleth over 66 Legions of Infernal Spirits. He appeareth in divers shapes, sometimes like a Cat, sometimes like a Toad, and sometimes like a Man, and sometimes all these forms at once. He speaketh hoarsely. This is his character which is used to be worn as a Lamen before him who calleth him forth, or else he will not do thee homage.

2. AGARES. The Second Spirit is a Duke called Agreas, or Agares. He is under the Power of the East, and cometh up in the form of an old fair Man, riding upon a Crocodile, carrying a Goshawk upon his fist, and yet mild in appearance. He maketh them to run that stand still, and bringeth back runaways. He teaches all Languages or Tongues presently. He hath power also to destroy Dignities both Spiritual and Temporal, and causeth Earthquakes. He was of the Order of Virtues. He hath under his government 31 Legions of Spirits. And this is his Seal or Character which thou shalt wear as a Lamen before thee.

3. VASSAGO. The Third Spirit is a Mighty Prince, being of the same nature as Agares. He is called Vassago. This Spirit is of a Good Nature, and his office is to declare things Past and to Come, and to discover all things Hid or Lost. And he governeth 26 Legions of Spirits, and this is his Seal.

4. SAMIGINA, or GAMIGIN. The Fourth Spirit is Samigina, a Great MarquIsaiah He appeareth in the form of a little Horse or Ass, and then into Human shape doth he change himself at the request of the Master. He speaketh with a hoarse voice. He ruleth over 30 Legions of Inferiors. He teaches all Liberal Sciences, and giveth account of Dead Souls that died in sin. And his Seal is this, which is to be worn before the Magician when he is Invocator, etc.

5. MARBAS. The fifth Spirit is Marbas. He is a Great President, and appeareth at first in the form of a Great Lion, but afterwards, at the request of the Master, he putteth on Human Shape. He answereth truly of things Hidden or Secret. He causeth Diseases and cureth them. Again, he giveth great Wisdom and Knowledge in Mechanical Arts; and can change men into other shapes. He governeth 36 Legions of Spirits. And his Seal is this, which is to be worn as aforesaid.

6. VALEFOR. The Sixth Spirit is Valefor. He is a mighty Duke, and appeareth in the shape of a Lion with an Ass's Head, bellowing. He is a good Familiar, but tempteth them he is a familiar of to steal. He governeth 10 Legions of Spirits. His Seal is this, which is to be worn, whether thou wilt have him for a Familiar, or not.

7. AMON. The Seventh Spirit is Amon. He is a Marquis great in power, and most stern. He appeareth like a Wolf with a Serpent's tail, vomiting out of his mouth flames of fire; but at the command of the Magician he putteth on the shape of a Man with Dog's teeth beset in a head like a Raven; or else like a Man with a Raven's head (simply). He telleth all things Past and to Come. He procureth feuds and reconcileth controversies between friends. He governeth 40 Legions of Spirits. His Seal is this which is to be worn as aforesaid, etc.

8. BARBATOS. The Eighth Spirit is Barbatos. He is a Great Duke, and appeareth when the Sun is in Sagittary, with four noble Kings and their companies of great troops. He giveth understanding of the singing of Birds, and of the Voices of other creatures, such as the barking of Dogs. He breaketh the Hidden Treasures open that have been laid by the Enchantments of Magicians. He is of the Order of Virtues, of which some part he retaineth still; and he knoweth all things Past, and to come, and conciliateth Friends and those that be in Power. He ruleth over 30 Legions of Spirits. His Seal of Obedience is this, the which wear before thee as aforesaid.

9. PAIMON. The Ninth Spirit in this Order is Paimon, a Great King, and very obedient unto LUCIFER. He appeareth in the form of a Man sitting upon a Dromedary with a Crown most glorious upon his head. There goeth before him also an Host of Spirits, like Men with Trumpets and well sounding Cymbals, and all other sorts of Musical Instruments. He hath a great Voice, and roareth at his first coming, and his speech is such that the Magician cannot well understand unless he can compel him. This Spirit can teach all Arts and Sciences, and other secret things. He can discover unto thee what the Earth is, and what holdeth it up in the Waters; and what Mind is, and where it is; or any other thing thou mayest desire to know. He giveth Dignity, and confirmeth the same. He

bindeth or maketh any man subject unto the Magician if he so desire it. He giveth good Familiars, and such as can teach all Arts. He is to be observed towards the West. He is of the Order of Dominations. He hath under him 200 Legions of Spirits, and part of them are of the Order of Angels, and the other part of Potentates. Now if thou callest this Spirit Paimon alone, thou must make him some offering; and there will attend him two Kings called LABAL and ABALI, and also other Spirits who be of the Order of Potentates in his Host, and 25 Legions. And those Spirits which be subject unto them are not always with them unless the Magician do compel them. His Character is this which must be worn as a Lamen before thee, etc.

10. BUER. The Tenth Spirit is Buer, a Great President. He appeareth in Sagittary, and that is his shape when the Sun is there. He teaches Philosophy, both Moral and Natural, and the Logic Art, and also the Virtues of all Herbs and Plants. He healeth all distempers in man, and giveth good Familiars. He governeth 50 Legions of Spirits, and his Character of obedience is this, which thou must wear when thou callest him forth unto appearance or Dominions, as they are usually termed.

11. GUSION. The Eleventh Spirit in order is a great and strong Duke, called Gusion. He appeareth like a Xenopilus. He telleth all things, Past, Present, and to Come, and showeth the meaning and resolution of all questions thou mayest ask. He conciliateth and reconcileth friendships, and giveth Honour and Dignity unto any. He ruleth over 40 Legions of Spirits. His Seal is this, the which wear thou as aforesaid.

12. SITRI. The Twelfth Spirit is Sitri. He is a Great Prince and appeareth at first with a Leopard's head and the Wings of a Gryphon, but after the command of the Master of the Exorcism he putteth on Human shape, and that very beautiful. He enflameth men with Women's love, and Women with Men's love; and causeth them also to show themselves naked if it be desired. He governeth 60 Legions of Spirits. His Seal is this, to be worn as a Lamen before thee, etc.

13. BELETH. The Thirteenth Spirit is called Beleth (or Bileth, or Bilet). He is a mighty King and terrible. He rideth on a pale horse with trumpets and other kinds of musical instruments playing before him. He is very

furious at his first appearance, that is, while the Exorcist layeth his courage; for to do this he must hold a Hazel Wand in his hand, striking it out towards the South and East Quarters, make a triangle, Ò, without the Circle, and then command him into it by the Bonds and Charges of Spirits as hereafter followeth. And if he doth not enter into the triangle, Ò, at your threats, rehearse the Bonds and Charms before him, and then he will yield Obedience and come into it, and do what he is commanded by the Exorcist. Yet he must receive him courteously because he is a Great King, and do homage unto him, as the Kings and Princes do that attend upon him. And thou must have always a Silver Ring on the middle finger of the left hand held against thy face, as they do yet before Amaymon. This Great King Beleth causeth all the love that may be, both of Men and of Women, until the Master Exorcist To protect him from the flaming breath of the enraged Spirit; the design is given at the end of the instructions for the Magical Circle, etc., later on in the Goetia. hath had his desire fulfilled. He is of the Order of Powers, and he governeth 85 Legions of Spirits. His Noble Seal is this, which is to be worn before thee at working.

14. Leraje, or Leraikha. The Fourteenth Spirit is called Leraje (or Leraie). He is a Marquis Great in Power, showing himself in the likeness of an Archer clad in Green, and carrying a Bow and Quiver. He causeth all great Battles and Contests; and maketh wounds to putrefy that are made with Arrows by Archers. This belongeth unto Sagittary. He governeth 30 Legions of Spirits, and this is his Seal, etc.

15. Eligos. The Fifteenth Spirit in Order is Eligos, a Great Duke, and appeareth in the form of a goodly Knight, carrying a Lance, an Ensign, and a Serpent. He discovereth hidden things, and knoweth things to come; and of Wars, and how the Soldiers will or shall meet. He causeth the Love of Lords and Great Persons. He governeth 60 Legions of Spirits. His Seal is this, etc.

16. Zepar. The Sixteenth Spirit is Zepar. He is a Great Duke, and appeareth in Red Apparel and Armour, like a Soldier. His office is to cause Women to love Men, and to bring them together in love. He also maketh them

barren. He governeth 26 Legions of Inferior Spirits, and his Seal is this, which he obeyeth when he seeth it.

17. BOTISAIAH. The Seventeenth Spirit is Botis, a Great President, and an Earl. He appeareth at the first show in the form of an ugly Viper, then at the command of the Magician he putteth on a Human shape with Great Teeth, and two Horns, carrying a bright and sharp Sword in his hand. He telleth all things Past, and to Come, and reconcileth Friends and Foes. He ruleth over 60 Legions of Spirits, and this is his Seal, etc.

18. BATHIN. The Eighteenth Spirit is Bathin. He is a Mighty and Strong Duke, and appeareth like a Strong Man with the tail of a Serpent, sitting upon a Pale-Coloured Horse. He knoweth the Virtues of Herbs and Precious Stones, and can transport men suddenly from one country to another. He ruleth over 30 Legions of Spirits. His Seal is this which is to be worn as aforesaid.

19. SALLOS. The Nineteenth Spirit is Sallos (or Saleos). He is a Great and Mighty Duke, and appeareth in the form of a gallant Soldier riding on a Crocodile, with a Ducal Crown on his head, but peaceably. He causeth the Love of Women to Men, and of Men to Women; and governeth 30 Legions of Spirits. His Seal is this, etc.

20. PURSON. The Twentieth Spirit is Purson, a Great King. His appearance is comely, like a Man with a Lion's face, carrying a cruel Viper in his hand, and riding upon a Bear. Going before him are many Trumpets sounding. He knoweth all things hidden, and can discover Treasure, and tell all things Past, Present, and to Come. He can take a Body either Human or Aërial, and answereth truly of all Earthly things both Secret and Divine, and of the Creation of the World. He bringeth forth good Familiars, and under his Government there be 22 Legions of Spirits, partly of the Order of Virtues and partly of the Order of Thrones. His Mark, Seal, or Character is this, unto the which he oweth obedience, and which thou shalt wear in time of action, etc.

21. MARAX. The Twenty-first Spirit is Marax. He is a Great Earl and President. He appeareth like a great Bull with a Man's face. His office is to make Men very knowing in Astronomy, and all other Liberal Sciences; also he can give good Familiars, and wise, knowing the virtues of Herbs

and Stones which be precious. He governeth 30 Legions of Spirits, and his Seal is this, which must be made and worn as aforesaid, etc.

22. IPOS. The Twenty-second Spirit is lpos. He is an Earl, and a Mighty Prince, and appeareth in the form of an Angel with a Lion's Head, and a Goose's Foot, and Hare's Tail. He knoweth all things Past, Present, and to Come. He maketh men witty and bold. He governeth 36 Legions of Spirits. His Seal is this, which thou shalt wear, etc,.

23. AIM. The Twenty-third Spirit is Aim. He is a Great Strong Duke. He appeareth in the form of a very handsome Man in body, but with three Heads; the first, like a Serpent, the second like a Man having two Stars on his Forehead, the third like a Calf. He rideth on a Viper, carrying a Firebrand in his Hand, wherewith he setteth cities, castles, and great Places, on fire. He maketh thee witty in all manner of ways, and giveth true answers unto private matters. He governeth 26 Legions of Inferior Spirits; and his Seal is this, which wear thou as aforesaid, etc.

24. NABERIUS. The Twenty-fourth Spirit is Naberius. He is a most valiant Marquis, and showeth in the form of a Black Crane, fluttering about the Circle, and when he speaketh it is with a hoarse voice. He maketh men cunning in all Arts and Sciences, but especially in the Art of Rhetoric. He restoreth lost Dignities and Honours. He governeth 19 Legions of Spirits. His Seal is this, which is to be worn, etc.

25. GLASYA-LABOLAS. The Twenty-fifth Spirit is Glasya-Labolas. He is a Mighty President and Earl, and showeth himself in the form of a Dog with Wings like a Gryphon. He teacheth all Arts and Sciences in an instant, and is an Author of Bloodshed and Manslaughter. He teacheth all things Past, and to Come. If desired he causeth the love both of Friends and of Foes. He can make a Man to go Invisible. And he hath under his command 36 Legions of Spirits. His Seal is this, to be, etc.

26. BUNE, or BIME. The Twenty-sixth Spirit is Bune (or Bim). He is a Strong, Great and Mighty Duke. He appeareth in the form of a Dragon with three heads, one like a Dog, one like a Gryphon, and one like a Man. He speaketh with a high and comely Voice. He changeth the Place of the Dead, and causeth the Spirits which be under him to gather together upon your Sepulchres. He giveth Riches unto a Man, and maketh him

Wise and Eloquent. He giveth true Answers unto Demands. And he governeth 30 Legions of Spirits. His Seal is this, unto the which he oweth Obedience. He hath another Seal (which is the first of these, but the last is the best).

27. RONOVE. The Twenty-seventh Spirit is Ronove. He appeareth in the Form of a Monster. He teacheth the Art of Rhetoric very well and giveth Good Servants, Knowledge of Tongues, and Favours with Friends or Foes. He is a Marquis and Great Earl; and there be under his command 19 Legions of Spirits. His Seal is this, etc.

28. BERITH. The Twenty-eighth Spirit in Order, as Solomon bound them, is named Berith. He is a Mighty, Great, and Terrible Duke. He hath two other Names given unto him by men of later times, viz.: BEALE, or BEAL, and BOFRY or BOLFRY. He appeareth in the Form of a Soldier with Red Clothing, riding upon a Red Horse, and having a Crown of Gold upon his head. He giveth true answers, Past, Present, and to Come. Thou must make use of a Ring in calling him forth, as is before spoken of regarding Beleth. He can turn all metals into Gold. He can give Dignities, and can confirm them unto Man. He speaketh with a very clear and subtle Voice. He governeth 26 Legions of Spirits. His Seal is this, etc.

29. ASTAROTH. The Twenty-ninth Spirit is Astaroth. He is a Mighty, Strong Duke, and appeareth in the Form of an hurtful Angel riding on an Infernal Beast like a Dragon, and carrying in his right hand a Viper. Thou must in no wise let im approach too near unto thee, lest he do thee damage by his Noisome Breath. Wherefore the Magician must hold the Magical Ring near his face, and that will defend him. He giveth true answers of things Past, Present, and to Come, and can discover all Secrets. He will declare wittingly how the Spirits fell, if desired, and the reason of his own fall. He can make men wonderfully knowing in all Liberal Sciences. He ruleth 40 Legions of Spirits. His Seal is this, which wear thou as a Lamen before thee, or else he will not appear nor yet obey thee, etc.

30. FORNEUS. The Thirtieth Spirit is Forneus. He is a Mighty and Great Marquis, and appeareth in the Form of a Great Sea Monster. He teacheth,

and maketh men wonderfully knowing in the Art of Rhetoric. He causeth men to have a good Name, and to have the knowledge and understanding of Tongues. He maketh one to be beloved of his Foes as well as of his Friends. He governeth 29 Legions of Spirits, partly of the Order of Thrones, and partly of that of Angels. His Seal is this, which wear thou, etc.

31. FORAS. The Thirty-first Spirit is Foras. He is a Mighty President, and appeareth in the Form of a Strong Man in Human Shape. He can give the understanding to Men how they may know the Virtues of all Herbs and Precious Stones. He teacheth the Arts of Logic and Ethics in all their parts. If desired he maketh men invisible, and to live long, and to be eloquent. He can discover Treasures and recover things Lost. He ruleth over 29 Legions of Spirits, and his Seal is this, which wear thou, etc.

32. ASMODAY. The Thirty-second Spirit is Asmoday, or Asmodai. He is a Great King, Strong, and Powerful. He appeareth with Three Heads, whereof the first is like a Bull, the second like a Man, and the third like a Ram; he hath also the tail of a Serpent, and from his mouth issue Flames of Fire. His Feet are webbed like those of a Goose. He sitteth upon an Infernal Dragon, and beareth in his hand a Lance with a Banner. He is first and choicest under the Power of AMAYMON, he goeth before all other. When the Exorcist hath a mind to call him, let it be abroad, and let him stand on his feet all the time of action, with his Cap or Headdress off; for if it be on, AMAYMON will deceive him and call all his actions to be bewrayed. But as soon as the Exorcist seeth Asmoday in the shape aforesaid, he shall call him by his Name, saying: "Art thou Asmoday?" and he will not deny it, and by-and-by he will bow down unto the ground. He giveth the Ring of Virtues; he teacheth the Arts of Arithmetic, Astronomy, Geometry, and all handicrafts absolutely. He giveth true and full answers unto thy demands. He maketh one Invincible. He showeth the place where Treasures lie, and guardeth it. He, amongst the Legions of AMAYMON governeth 72 Legions of Spirits Inferior. His Seal is this which thou must wear as a Lamen upon thy breast, etc.

33. GAAP. The Thirty-third Spirit is Gaap. He is a Great President and a Mighty Prince. He appeareth when the Sun is in some of the Southern Signs, in a Human Shape, going before Four Great and Mighty Kings, as if lie were a Guide to conduct them along on their way. His Office is to make men Insensible or Ignorant; as also in Philosophy to make them Knowing, and in all the Liberal Sciences. He can cause Love or Hatred, also he can teach thee to consecrate those things that belong to the Dominion of AMAYMON his King. He can deliver Familiars out of the Custody of other Magicians, and answereth truly and perfectly of things Past, Present, and to Come. He can carry and recarry men very speedily from one Kingdom to another, at the Will and Pleasure of the Exorcist. He ruleth over 66 Legions of Spirits, and he was of the Order of Potentates. His Seal is this to be made and to be worn as aforesaid, etc.

34. FURFUR. The Thirty-fourth Spirit is Furfur. He is a Great and Mighty Earl, appearing in the Form of an Hart with a Fiery Tail. He never speaketh truth unless he be compelled, or brought up within a triangle. Being therein, he will take upon himself the Form of an Angel. Being bidden, he speaketh with a hoarse voice. Also he will wittingly urge Love between Man and Woman. He can raise Lightnings and Thunders, Blasts, and Great Tempestuous Storms. And he giveth True Answers both of Things Secret and Divine, if commanded. He ruleth over 26 Legions of Spirit and his Seal is this, etc.

35. MARCHOSIAS. The Thirty-fifth Spirit is Marchosias. He is a Great and Mighty Marquis, appearing at first in the Form of a Wolf having Gryphon's Wings, and a Serpent's Tail, and Vomiting Fire out of his mouth. But after a time, at the command of the Exorcist he putteth on the Shape of a Man. And he is a strong fighter. He was of the Order of Dominations. He governeth 30 Legions of Spirits. He told his Chief, who was Solomon, that after 1,200 years he had hopes to return unto the Seventh Throne. And his Seal is this, to be made and worn as a Lamen, etc.

36. STOLAS, or STOLOS. The Thirty-sixth Spirit is Stolas, or Stolos. He is a Great and Powerful Prince, appearing in the Shape of a Mighty Raven at first before the Exorcist; but after he taketh the image of a Man. He

teacheth the Art of Astronomy, and the Virtues of Herbs and Precious Stones. He governeth 26 Legions of Spirits; and his Seal is this, which is, etc.

37. PHENEX. The Thirty-Seventh Spirit is Phenex (or Pheynix). He is a great Marquis, and appeareth like the Bird Phoenix, having the Voice of a Child. He singeth many sweet notes before the Exorcist, which he must not regard, but by-and-by he must bid him put on Human Shape. Then he will speak marvellously of all wonderful Sciences if required. He is a Poet, good and excellent. And he will be willing to perform thy requests. He hath hopes also to return to the Seventh Throne after 1,200 years more, as he said unto Solomon. He governeth 20 Legions of Spirits. And his Seal is this, which wear thou, etc.

38. HALPHAS, or MALTHUS. The Thirty-eighth Spirit is Halphas, or Malthous (or Malthas). He is a Great Earl, and appeareth in the Form of a Stock-Dove. He speaketh with a hoarse Voice. His Office is to build up Towers, and to furnish them with Ammunition and Weapons, and to send Men-of-War to places appointed. He ruleth over 26 Legions of Spirits, and his Seal is this, etc.

39. MALPHAS. The Thirty-ninth Spirit is Malphas. He appeareth at first like a Crow, but after he will put on Human Shape at the request of the Exorcist, and speak with a hoarse Voice. He is a Mighty President and Powerful. He can build Houses and High Towers, and can bring to thy Knowledge Enemies' Desires and Thoughts, and that which they have done. He giveth Good Familiars. If thou makest a Sacrifice unto him he will receive it kindly and willingly, but he will deceive him- that doth it. He governeth 40 Legions of Spirits, and his Seal is this, etc. Or Warriors, or Men-at-Arms.

40. RAUM. The Fortieth Spirit is Raum. He is a Great Earl; and appeareth at first in the Form of a Crow, but after the Command of the Exorcist he putteth on Human Shape. His office is to steal Treasures out King's Houses, and to carry it whither he is commanded, and to destroy Cities and Dignities of Men, and to tell all things, Past and What Is, and what Will Be; and to cause Love between Friends and Foes. He was of the

Order of Thrones. He governeth 30 Legions of Spirits; and his Seal is this, which wear thou as aforesaid.

41. FOCALOR. The Forty-first Spirit is Focalor, or Forcalor, or Furcalor. He is a Mighty Duke and Strong. He appeareth in the Form of a Man with Gryphon's Wings. His office is to slay Men, and to drown them in the Waters, and to overthrow Ships of War, for he hath Power over both Winds and Seas; but he will not hurt any man or thing if he be commanded to the contrary by the Exorcist. He also hath hopes to return to the Seventh Throne after 1,000 years. He governeth 30 Legions of Spirits, and his Seal is this, etc.

42. VEPAR. The Forty-second Spirit is Vepar, or Vephar. He is a Duke Great and Strong and appeareth like a Mermaid. His office is to govern the Waters, and to guide Ships laden with Arms, Armour, and Ammunition, etc., thereon. And at the request of the Exorcist he can cause the seas to be right stormy and to appear full of ships. Also he maketh men to die in Three Days by Putrefying Wounds or Sores, and causing Worms to breed in them. He governeth 29 Legions of Spirits, and his Seal is this, etc.

43. SABNOCK. The Forty-third Spirit, as King Solomon commanded them into the Vessel of Brass, is called Sabnock, or Savnok. He is a Marquis, Mighty, Great and Strong, appearing in the Form of an Armed Soldier with a Lion's Head, riding on a pale-coloured horse. His office is to build high Towers, Castles and Cities, and to furnish them with Armour, etc. Also he can afflict Men for many days with Wounds and with Sores rotten and full of Worms. He giveth Good Familiars at the request of the Exorcist. He commandeth 50 Legions of Spirits; and his Seal is thIsaiah

44. SHAN. The Forty-fourth Spirit is Shax, or Shaz (or Shass). He is a Great Marquis and appeareth in the Form of a Stock-Dove, speaking with a voice hoarse, but yet subtle. His Office is to take away the Sight, Hearing, or Understanding of any Man or Woman at the command of the Exorcist; and to steal money out of the houses of Kings, and to carry it again in 1,200 years. If commanded he will fetch Horses at the request of the Exorcist, or any other thing. But he must first be commanded into a Triangle, or else he will deceive him, and tell him many Lies. He can discover all things that are Hidden, and not kept by Wicked Spirits. He

giveth good Familiars, sometimes. He governeth 30 Legions of Spirits, and his Seal is this, etc.

45. VINE. The Forty-fifth Spirit is Vine, or Vinea. He is a Great King, and an Earl; and appeareth in the Form of a Lion, riding upon a Black Horse, and bearing a Viper in his hand. His Office is to discover Things Hidden, Witches, Wizards, and Things Present, Past, and to Come. He, at the command of the Exorcist will build Towers, overthrow Great Stone Walls, and make the Waters rough with Storms. He governeth 36 Legions of Spirits. And his Seal is this, which wear thou, as aforesaid, etc.

46. BIFRONS. The Forty-sixth Spirit is called Bifrons, or Bifrous, or Bifrovs. He is an Earl, and appeareth in the Form of a Monster; but after a while, at the Command of the Exorcist, he putteth on the shape of a Man. His Office is to make one knowing in Astrology, Geometry, and other Arts and Sciences. He teacheth the Virtues of Precious Stones and Woods. He changeth Dead Bodies, and putteth them in another place; also he lighteth seeming Candles upon the Graves of the Dead. He hath under his Command 6 Legions of Spirits. His Seal is this, which he will own and submit unto, etc.

47. UVALL, VUAL, or VOVAL. The Forty-seventh Spirit Uvall, or Vual, or Voval. He is a Duke, Great, Mighty, and Strong; and appeareth in the Form of a Mighty Dromedary at the first, but after a while at the Command of the Or "with the Head of a Lion," or "having a Lion his Head," in some Codices. Exorcist he putteth on Human Shape, and speaketh the Egyptian Tongue, but not perfectly. His Office is to procure the Love of Woman, and to tell Things Past, Present, and to Come. He also procureth Friendship between Friends and Foes. He was of the Order of Potestates or Powers. He governeth 37 Legions of Spirits, and his Seal is this, to be made and worn before thee, etc.

48. HAAGENTI. The Forty-eighth Spirit is Haagenti. He is a President, appearing in the Form of a Mighty Bull with Gryphon's Wings. This is at first, but after, at the Command of the Exorcist he putteth on Human Shape. His Office is to make Men wise, and to instruct them in divers things; also to Transmute all Metals into Gold; and to change Wine

into Water, and Water into Wine. He governeth 33 Legions of Spirits, and his Seal is this, etc.

49. CROCELL. The Forty-ninth Spirit is Crocell, or Crokel. He appeareth in the Form of an Angel. He is a Duke Great and Strong, speaking something Mystically of Hidden Things. He teacheth the Art of Geometry and the Liberal Sciences. He, at the Command of the Exorcist, will produce Great Noises like the Rushings of many Waters, although there be none. He warmeth Waters, and discovereth Baths. He was of the Order of Potestates, or Powers, before his fall, as he declared unto the King Solomon. He governeth 48 Legions of Spirits. His Seal is this, the which wear thou as aforesaid.

50. FURCAS. The Fiftieth Spirit is Furcas. He is a Knight, and appeareth in the Form of a Cruel Old Man with a long Beard and a hoary Head, riding upon a pale-coloured Horse, with a Sharp Weapon in his hand. His Office is to teach the Arts of Philosophy, Astrology, Rhetoric, Logic, Cheiromancy, and Pyromancy, in all their parts, and perfectly. He hath under his Power 20 Legions of Spirits. His Seal, or Mark, is thus made, etc. He can nowadays converse in sound though colloquial Coptic.

51. BALAM. The Fifty-first Spirit is Balam or Balaam. He is a Terrible, Great, and Powerful King. He appeareth with three Heads: the first is like that of a Bull; the second is like that of a Man; the third is like that of a Ram. He hath the Tail of a Serpent, and Flaming Eyes. He rideth upon a furious Bear, and carrieth a Boshawk upon his Fist. He speaketh with a hoarse Voice, giving True Answers of Things Past, Present, and to Come. He maketh men to go Invisible, and also to be Witty. He governeth 40 Legions of Spirits. His Seal is this, etc.

52. ALLOCES. The Fifty-second Spirit is Alloces, or Alocas. He is a Duke, Great, Mighty, and Strong, appearing in the Form of a Soldier riding upon a Great Horse. His Face is like that of a Lion, very Red, and having Flaming Eyes. His Speech is hoarse and very big. His Office is to teach the Art of Astronomy, and all the Liberal Sciences. He bringeth unto thee Good Familiars; also he ruleth over 36 Legions of Spirits. His Seal is this, which, etc.

53. CAMIO or CAIM. The Fifty-third Spirit is Camio, or Caim. He is a Great President, and appeareth in the Form of the Bird called a Thrush at first, but afterwards he putteth on the Shape of a Man carrying in his Hand a Sharp Sword. He seemeth to answer in Burning Ashes, or in Coals of Fire. He is a Good Disputer. His Office is to give unto Men the Understanding of all Birds, Lowing of Bullocks, Barking of Dogs, and other Creatures; and also of the Voice of the Waters. He giveth True Answers of Things to Come. He was of the Order of Angels, but now ruleth over 30 Legions of Spirits Infernal. His Seal is this, which wear thou, etc.

54. MURMUR, or MURMUS. The Fifty-fourth Spirit is called Murmur, or Murmus, or Murmux. He is a Great Duke, and an Earl; and appeareth in the Form of a Warrior riding upon a. Gryphon, with a Ducal Crown upon his Head. There do go before him those his Ministers, with great Trumpets sounding. His Office is to teach Philosophy perfectly, and to constrain Souls Or Warrior. Thus expressed in the Codices. Deceased to come before the Exorcist to answer those questions which he may wish to put to them, if desired. He was partly of the Order of Thrones, and partly of that of Angels. He now ruleth 30 Legions of Spirits. And his Seal is this, etc.

55. OROBAS. The Fifty-fifth Spirit is Orobas. He is a great and Mighty Prince, appearing at first like a Horse; but after the command of the Exorcist he putteth on the Image of a Man. His Office is to discover all things Past, Present, and to Come; also to give Dignities, and Prelacies, and the Favour of Friends and of Foes. He giveth True Answers of Divinity, and of the Creation of the World. He is very faithful unto the Exorcist, and will not suffer him to be tempted of any Spirit. He governeth 20 Legions of Spirits. His Seal is this, etc.

56. GREMORY, or GAMORI. The Fifty-sixth Spirit is Gremory, or Gamori. He is a Duke Strong and Powerful, and appeareth in the Form of a Beautiful Woman, with a Duchess's Crown tied about her waist, and riding on a Great Camel. His Office is to tell of all Things Past, Present, and to Come; and of Treasures Hid, and what they lie in; and to procure

the Love of Women both Young and Old. He governeth 26 Legions of Spirits, and his Seal is this, etc.

57. OSE, or VOSO. The Fifty-seventh Spirit is Oso, Ose, or Voso. He is a Great President, and appeareth like a Leopard at the first, but after a little time he putteth on the Shape of a Man. His Office is to make one cunning in the Liberal Sciences, and to give True Answers of Divine and Secret Things; also to change a Man into any Shape that the Exorcist pleaseth so that he that is so changed will not think any other thing than that he is in verity that Creature or Thing he is changed into. He governeth 3024 Legions of Spirits, and this is his Seal, etc.

58. AMY, or AVNAS. The Fifty-eighth Spirit is Amy, or Avnas. He is a Great President, and appeareth at first in the Form of a Flaming Fire; but after a while he putteth on the Shape of a Man. His office is to make one Wonderful Knowing in Astrology and all the Liberal Sciences. He giveth Good Familiars, and can bewray Treasure that is kept by Spirits. He governeth 36 Legions of Spirits, and his Seal is this, etc.

59. ORIAX, or ORIAS. The Fifty-ninth Spirit is Oriax, or Orias. He is a Great Marquis, and appeareth in the Form of a Lion, riding upon a Horse Mighty and Strong, with a Serpent's Tail; and he holdeth in his Right Hand two Great Serpents hissing. His Office is to teach the Virtues of the Stars, and to know the Mansions of the Planets, and how to understand their Virtues. He also transformeth Men, and he giveth Dignities, Prelacies, and Confirmation thereof; also Favour with Friends and with Foes. He doth govern 30 Legions of Spirits; and his Seal is this, etc.

60. VAPULA, or NAPHULA. The Sixtieth Spirit is Vapula, or Naphula. He is a Duke Great, Mighty, and Strong; appearing in the Form of a. Lion with Gryphon's Wings. His Office is to make Men Knowing in all Handcrafts and Professions, also in Philosophy, and other Sciences. He governeth 36 Legions of Spirits, and his Seal or Character is thus made, and thou shalt wear it as aforesaid, etc.

61. ZAGAN. The Sixty-first Spirit is Zagan. He is a Great King and President, appearing at first in the Form of a Bull with Gryphon's Wings; but after a while he putteth on Human Shape. He maketh Men Witty. He can turn Wine into Water, and Blood into Wine, also Water into Wine.

He can turn all Metals into Coin of the Dominion that Metal is of. He can even make Fools wise. He governeth 33 Legions of Spirits, and his Seal is this, etc.

62. VOLAC, or VALAK, or VALU, or VALAC. The Sixty-second Spirit is Volac, or Valak, or Valu. He is a President Mighty and Great, and appeareth like a Child with Angel's Wings, riding on a Two-headed Dragon. His Office is to Thus in the actual Text. Or "with the Face of a Lion." give True Answers of Hidden Treasures, and to tell where Serpents may be seen. The which he will bring unto the Exorciser without any Force or Strength being by him employed. He governeth 38 Legions of Spirits, and his Seal is thus.

63. ANDRAS. The Sixty-third Spirit is Andras. He is a Great Marquis, appearing in the Form of an Angel with a Head like a Black Night Raven, riding upon a strong Black Wolf, and having a Sharp and Bright Sword flourished aloft in his hand. His Office is to sow Discords. If the Exorcist have not a care, he will slay both him and his fellows. He governeth 30 Legions of Spirits, and this is his Seal, etc.

64. HAURES, or HAURAS, or HAVRES, or FLAUROB. The Sixty-fourth Spirit is Haures, or Hauras, or Havres, or Flauros. He is a Great Duke, and appeareth at first like a Leopard, Mighty, Terrible, and Strong, but after a while, at the Command of the Exorcist, he putteth on Human. Shape with Eyes Flaming and Fiery, and a most Terrible Countenance. He giveth True Answers of all things, Present, Past, and to Come. But if he be not commanded into a Triangle, he will Lie in all these Things, and deceive and beguile the Exorcist in these things, or in such and such business. He will, lastly, talk of the Creation of the World, and of Divinity, and of how he and other Spirits fell. He destroyeth and burneth up those who be the Enemies of the Exorcist should he so desire it; also he will not suffer him to be tempted by any other Spirit or otherwise. He governeth 36 Legions of Spirits, and his Seal is this, to be worn as a Lamen, etc.

65. ANDREALPHUS. The Sixty-fifth Spirit is Andrealphus. He is a Mighty Marquis, appearing at first in the form of a Peacock, with great Noises. But after a time he putteth on Human shape. He can teach Geometry

perfectly. He maketh Men very subtle therein; and in all Things pertaining unto Mensuration or Astronomy. He can transform a Man into the Likeness of a Bird. He governeth 30 Legions of Infernal Spirits, and his Seal is this, etc.

66. CIMEJES, or CIMEIES, or KIMARISAIAH. The Sixtysixth Spirit is Cimejes, or Cimeies, or KimarIsaiah He is a Marquis, Mighty, Great, Strong and Powerful, appearing like a Valiant Warrior riding upon a goodly Black Horse. He ruleth over all Spirits in the parts of Africa. His Office is to teach perfectly Grammar, Logic, Rhetoric, and to discover things Lost or Hidden, and Treasures. He governeth 20 Legions of Infernals; and his Seal is this, etc.

67. AMDUSIAS, or AMDUKIAS. The Sixty-seventh Spirit is Amdusias, or Amdukias. He is a Duke Great and Strong, appearing at first like a Unicorn, but at the request of the Exorcist he standeth before him in Human Shape, causing Trumpets, and all manner of Musical Instruments to be heard, but not soon or immediately. Also he can cause Trees to bend and incline according to the Exorcist's Will. He giveth Excellent Familiars. He governeth 29 Legions of Spirits. And his Seal is this, etc.

68. BELIAL. The Sixty-eighth Spirit is Belial. He is a Mighty and a Powerful King, and was created next after LUCIFER. He appeareth in the Form of Two Beautiful Angels sitting in a Chariot of Fire. He speaketh with a Comely Voice, and declareth that he fell first from among the worthier sort, that were before Michael, and other Heavenly Angels. His Office is to distribute Presentations and Senatorships, etc.; and to cause favour of Friends and of Foes. He giveth excellent Familiars, and governeth 50 Legions of Spirits. Note well that this King Belial must have Offerings, Sacrifices and Gifts presented unto him by the Exorcist, or else he will not give True Answers unto his Demands. But then he tarrieth not one hour in the Truth, unless he be constrained by Divine Power. And his Seal is this, which is to be worn as aforesaid, etc.

69. DECARABIA. The Sixty-ninth Spirit is Decarabia. He appeareth in the Form of a Star in a Pentacle, at first; but after, at the command of the Exorcist, he putteth on the image of a Man. His Office is to discover the Virtues of Birds and Precious Stones, and to make the Similitude

of all kinds of Birds to fly before the Exorcist, singing and drinking as natural Birds do. He governeth 30 Legions of Spirits, being himself a Great MarquIsaiah And this is his Seal, which is to be worn, etc.

70. SEERE, SEAR, or SEIR. The Seventieth Spirit is Seere, Sear, or Seir. He is a Mighty Prince, and Powerful, under AMAYMON, King of the East. He appeareth in the Form of a Beautiful Man, riding upon a Winged Horse. His Office is to go and come; and to bring abundance of things to pass on a sudden, and to carry or recarry anything whither thou wouldest have it to go, or whence thou wouldest have it from. He can pass over the whole Earth in the twinkling of an Eye. He giveth a True relation of all sorts of Theft, and of Treasure hid, and of many other things. He is of an indifferent Good Nature, and is willing to do anything which the Exorcist desireth. He governeth 26 Legions of Spirits. And this his Seal is to be worn, etc.

71. DANTALION. The Seventy-First Spirit is Dantalion. He is a Duke Great and Mighty, appearing in the Form of a Man with many Countenances, all Men's and Women's Faces; and he hath a Book in his right hand. His Office is to teach all Arts and Sciences unto any; and to declare the Secret Counsel of any one; for he knoweth the Thoughts of all Men and Women, and can change them at his Will. He can cause Love, and show the Similitude of any person, and show the same by a Vision, let them be in what part of the World they Will. He governeth 36 Legions of Spirits; and this is his Seal, which wear thou, etc.

72. ANDROMALIUS. The Seventy-second Spirit in Order is named Andromalius. He is an Earl, Great and Mighty, appearing in the Form of a Man holding a Great Serpent in his Hand. His Office is to bring back both a Thief, and the Goods which be stolen; and to discover all Wickedness, and Underhand Dealing; and to punish all Thieves and other Wicked People and also to discover Treasures that be Hid. He ruleth over 36 Legions of Spirits. His Seal is this, the which wear thou as aforesaid, etc.

THESE be the 72 Mighty Kings and Princes which King Solomon Commanded into a Vessel of Brass, together with their Legions. Of whom

BELIAL, BILETH, ASMODAY, and GAAP, were Chief. And it is to be noted that Solomon did this because of their pride, for he never declared other reason why he thus bound them. And when he had thus bound them up and sealed the Vessel, he by Divine Power did chase them all into a deep Lake or Hole in Babylon. And they of Babylon, wondering to see such a thing, they did then go wholly into the Lake, to break the Vessel open, expecting to find great store of Treasure therein. But when they had broken it open, out flew the Chief Spirits immediately, with their Legions following them; and they were all restored to their former places except BELIAL, who entered into a certain Image, and thence gave answers unto those who did offer Sacrifices unto him, and did worship the Image as their God, etc.

Chaos Magick

In Chaos Magick, Sigils are often created by writing out the intention, then condensing the letters of the statement to form a sort of cipher. The Chaos Magickian then uses the gnostic state to launch or charge the Sigil, essentially bypassing the conscious mind to implant the desire into the unconscious. The implications for this strategy are boundless.

The Chaos Magickian acknowledges a desire, he lists the appropriate symbols and arranges them into an easily visualized glyph. Using any of the gnostic techniques, he reifies the Sigil and then, by force of will, hurls it into his subconscious from where the Sigil can begin to work unencumbered by desire."

Afterward, the implied action is to force yourself to forget ever having created the Sigil. In Chaos Magick, when a myriad of thoughts, desires, and intentions gain such a level of sophistication, it appears to operate autonomously from the Magickian's consciousness, as if it were an independent being, accomplishing your goal, separately and synonymously with you. This is much like the cases involving your Alterna Unu, but applied on a conscious level and in a much smaller event.

Magickal traditions like Wicca, Qabalah or the Golden Dawn systems combine techniques for bringing about change with belief and Universal or

Cosmic Energy, a more freeform, improvisational method, stripping away all of the extraneous elements of memorizing complex rules and symbols and, then having to retain those rules and/or techniques and symbols to produce results. This leaves behind only the techniques for effecting change to the will of the user.

As the Satanic Order av Wyrd and their Satan are utmost advocates of Chaos, Chaos Magick directly corresponds with our operation. Furthermore, we do find these methods quite effective. We especially find these methods effective when applied to altering your own personal Cosmic Energy field. For example, consider the following:

Atavistic Nostalgia

The fundamental theory behind Atavistic Nostalgia is Darwin's theory of evolution: that man is but the momentary end-product of a long process of evolution that has been going on for millions of years. This process originated from unicellular organisms and gradually became reptiles and mammals, and insects, and us, the human race, and so on. Furthermore, unlike popular vulgar Darwinism, excessively monitored by the Church, Darwin did not so much claim that man derives from apes, as much as he alleged to the concept that we carry in us the entire heritage of all life forms and that we literally incorporate it into our daily dealings with everything and everyone.

The secondary or associated theory behind Atavistic Nostalgia, the more crucial component in respect to the practice of Atavistic Nostalgia, as perpetuated by Austin Osman Spare (appropriator of Chaos Magick and Atavistic Nostalgia), is that one needs to go back into early, prehuman stages of consciousness by activating genetic or hereditary memory. This, for Spare, was a tap, as his firm belief declared that our greatest Magickal power, even the source of magic itself, lay hidden in these early stages of evolution. This is a concept akin to the Satanic Order av Wyrd's beliefs that establishing a foundation and learning your roots is imperative to our way of life.

One should consider a few things before using Chaos Magick applied to Atavistic Nostalgia. One should have a great deal of Magickal experience prior to use. One should also have a strong mind, able to withstand what's necessary and able to navigate the psychic/psychological labyrinth that one may be forced to endure when dealing with such a Magickal process: With Atavistic Nostalgia, we enter prehuman stages of life, which, when introduced to the conscious mind, may have catastrophic results. You might come to the realization that your whole world view and all your usual ideas about morals and ethics have been drastically changed. You might be completely overwhelmed by your animal-consciousness or even become obsessed with your animal-consciousness. This could result in particularly unpleasant consequences in conventional society.

On the contrary, if one is successful, you'll be accomplishing something very similar to that of merging with your Alterna Unu, falling in line with the views of Carl Jung and many others. You will have accomplished something with which only few can identify. You'll be that much closer to knowing yourself to such an extent that you will have set yourself apart from the human race, becoming more superhuman, for lack of a better term, closer to a god, in essence!

Spare didn't leave precise directions on how to use Chaos Magick applied to Atavistic Nostalgia, but his Magickal pictures and Steles, in which he usually added handwritten explanations and observations, give us some idea about his methods. Of course, he achieved these changes in consciousness through the use of Sigils. But, first, as is customary for Chaos Magick, one must complete a preliminary exercise.

***

There are other methods for the aforementioned preliminary exercise. The method employed by tThe Satanic Order av Wyrd is known as Ecstatic gGnosis.is. Ecstatic Gnosis is a mindlessness or state of thoughtlessness reached through intense arousal. It is to be reached through sexual excitation, intense emotion, flagellation, dance, drumming, chanting, sensory overload, hyperventilation and/or the use of uninhibiting hallucinogenic substances. But, regardless of the method, the sole purpose of this exercise is to clear your mind, free yourself of thought, and put yourself in a state of euphoric short-term blissful trance.

There are several methods of Atavistic Nostalgia. We may shift our consciousness into that of different animals by constructing and activating proper sigils. The way we do this is to write out a Sentence of Desire pertaining to the animal with which you wish to pull forth and connect.

In SOW, we prefer to identify the animal that resonates the most with your characteristics and overall personality or way of being, as well as your appearance and mannerisms. This makes for a much more effective outcome. You may be already aware of the animal, due to your own personal observations and/or perceptions, as well as the observations of others. Others may have said, in passing or as a result of some interesting conversation, that you remind them of a wolf, or a hawk, or a lizard, or, in my case, a serpent.

The Sentence of Desire should be written while in that state induced by Ecstatic Gnosis on a piece of virgin parchment. The only words your mind should speak are the words contained within your Sentence of Desire. The following are some examples:

- **This my will to obtain the consciousness and abilities of a serpent.**
- **This my will to obtain the consciousness and abilities of a monkey.**
- **I want to experience all that is the tiger.**

Once you've written your Sentence of Desire, prick your left forefinger with your ritual dagger, just enough to make a streak of blood from the beginning to the end of the sentence. While applying the blood streak, read the sentence aloud as you pass over each word. This binds you to the Sentence of Desire.

After this, you are no longer required to maintain your Ecstatic Gnosis state. You may, however reenter, when the time comes to compile your characters into the Atavistic Nostalgia Sigil or seal. This will be addressed following the next few paragraphs.

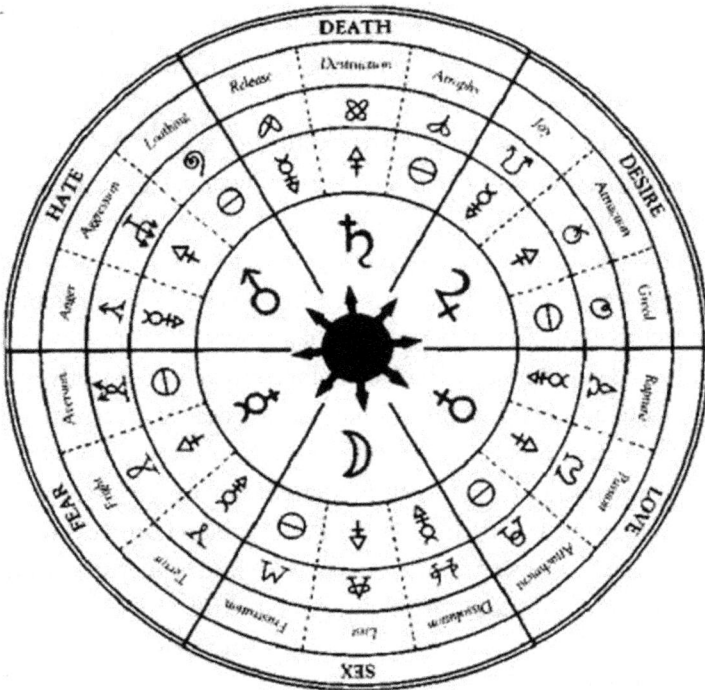

Some may prefer to use the Alphabet of Desire (for more information, refer to works by Spare or the Liber Null, etc.). If you wish to incorporate this into your ritual, by all means do so. Your Sigil work will then be bolstered that much more. But if you wish to proceed without the use of the Alphabet of Desire, the standard SOW adaptation will suffice.

From your Sentence of Desire, extract the individual letters, disregarding any duplicates. For example, take the sentence, "Rape and destroy the righteous!" You would take *r, a, p, e, n, d, s, t, o, y, h, i, g,* and *u* out of the sentence.

It is not necessary to use English. In fact, you can use any language. Furthermore, as the Alphabet of Desire would have it, you may even use phonetic characters of your Magickal creation. A typical phonetic (but not limited to phonetics) structure for the Satanic Order av Wyrd is the Elder Futhark.

In this stage of the process, you may reenter the Ecstatic Gnosis state. Throughout the duration of this stage, you will repeat your Sentence of Desire as a mantra, until the Sigil or seal is complete. Now, you'll create your Atavistic Nostalgia Sigil or seal.

On a new piece of virgin parchment, draw a circle. Within the circle, you will combine your extracted letters or characters, creating a completely new symbol or character. This new symbol, character, Sigil, seal, is your finished product and should look something like this:

The final stage in this exercise is to burn your Atavistic Nostalgia Sigil. We prefer to do this within our Ritual or Ceremonial Offering Bowl. Continue repeating your Sentence of Desire until it is reduced to ash. Then resort to whatever method possible to forget ever having created your Sigil. This is easier to do when emerging from your Ecstatic Gnosis state. But, if you need to add insult to injury, take shots of a strong alcohol, smoke marijuana, consume any other substance, until you're confident in the inevitability that the memory will be lost.

Germanic and Norse Sigils or Staves

Germanic and/or Norse Sigils, or both, typically, but not confined to, Icelandic Staves, are commonly referred to as Galdrastafir (refer to various texts or go online, if you require more information). Each Stave or Sigil has its own name and attributes or purpose and is often created using the Futharks, like the elder or younger Futharks below. We in SOW prefer the Elder Futhark for most of our Magickal dealings.

Elder Futhark

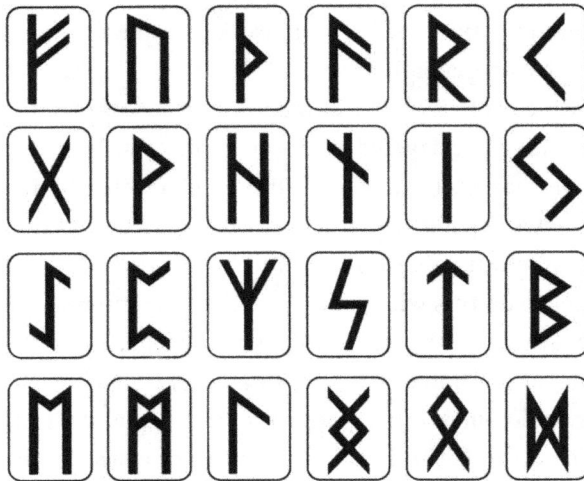

ᚠ ᚢ ᚦ ᚨ ᚱ ᚲ
ᚷ ᚹ ᚺ ᚾ ᛁ ᛃ
ᛇ ᛈ ᛉ ᛊ ᛏ ᛒ
ᛖ ᛗ ᛚ ᛜ ᛟ ᛞ

The Younger Futhark Runes

Danish (long branch) Futhark

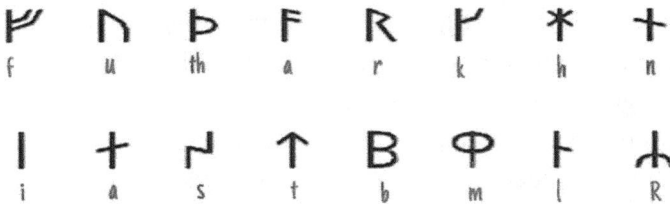

ᚠ	ᚢ	ᚦ	ᚨ	ᚱ	ᚴ	ᚼ	ᚾ
f	u	th	a	r	k	h	n

ᛁ	ᛆ	ᛋ	ᛏ	ᛒ	ᛘ	ᛚ	ᛦ
i	a	s	t	b	m	l	R

Swedish-Norwegian (Short-twig) Rök Runes

ᚠ	ᚢ	ᚦ	ᚨ	ᚱ	ᚴ	ᚽ	ᚿ
f	u	th	a	r	k	h	n

ᛁ	ᛅ	ᛌ	ᛐ	ᛓ	ᛙ	ᛚ	ᛧ
i	a	s	t	b	m	l	R

The following Sigils are predominately Galdrastafir with their names and attributes or purposes, some to which you are already acquainted. Please note that there are multiple methods of application for many of these. Additional steps may be required to ensure the power of each.

The Aegishjalmur or Helm of Awe

Make a helm of awe in lead, press the lead sign between the eyebrows, and speak the formula:

Ægishjálm er ég ber
milli brúna mér!
I bear the helm of awe
between my brows!

Thus a man could meet his enemies and be sure of victory.

Strength. Protection. Strike fear in your enemies. Victory in battle.

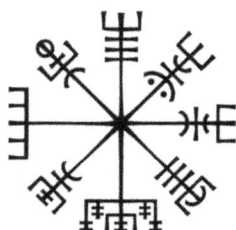

The Vegvisir

Whoever wears this Seal will travel the right path even if the destination is unknown. This is meant geographically, spiritually, and similarly.

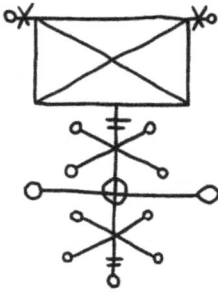

Stafur til að vekja upp draug
To call upon evil spirits or entities.

Gungnir
Power. Protection. Authority. This Seal can lead you to the All-father, Odin.

The Valknut
A guide for the transition between life and death, a symbol of those who fell in battle.

The Sun Wheel, The Black Sun, The Sun Cross, and/or The Swastika

The Swastika is commonly associated with the Nazi Party of Germany in the mid-twentieth century CE. However, it is actually an ancient symbol, that shares the same or similar meanings of the Sun Wheel/Black Sun and associated symbols, of power, holiness, prosperity, continuity, luck, and fire, the life-force, if you will, which appears in the iconography of many different cultures and religions around the world. Although it is most common in the Germanic cultures and their branches, such as the Norse.

The Web av Wyrd

Favorable assistance with the past, present, and future.

All of the Elder Futhark is contained within the Web.

Also a representation of the nine realms.

Yggdrasil

Assists in the connection between all things and the cyclical nature of life,

As well as the interconnectivity of the universe, much like Eiwhaz.

The Svefnthorn

The Svefnthorn or Sleep Thorn is meant for those of your enemies you wish to put into a deep, undisturbed sleep at length.

The following is the Enochian alphabet, a form of Sigil work. It is composed of twenty-two characters thought to make up the language of the angels.

Enochian is an occult language or languages recorded in the private journals of John Dee and his colleague Edward Kelley in late sixteenth-century England. Kelley was a spirit medium who worked with Dee in his magical investigations. The men claimed that the language was revealed to them by the Enochian Angels. The language is integral to the practice of Enochian Magick.

You may choose to use these characters in your general Magickal dealings and Sigil work. You may even feel inclined to familiarize yourself with Enochian Magick. We in the Satanic Order av Wyrd use them for their sentimental and aged value, often perverting them as we see fit, as to scorn the distinct Christian connotations.

The Confidential Order av Wyrd

Everything shared within this chapter is accessible only because the rituals, ceremonies, and Magick are practiced by a myriad of organizations and practitioners from all over the world that have made their knowledge public and easily accessible. We take pleasure in these collective traditions. However, this is merely a drop in the bucket compared to the practices, beliefs, traditions, politics, radical objectives, and the general mission of the Satanic Order av Wyrd.

In order to access the full benefits and practices of our organizations, you must become a member. The details of initiation and associated protocols and procedures will be covered at the end of this manuscript. We thank you for your consideration and look forward to interacting with you in the future.

CHAPTER VIII

The Vaesen and the Fae

All things considered, it wasn't really that long ago that mankind believed. In fact, we didn't have to believe, because it was reality, truth. No one knew any different. We coexisted with elemental creatures, spiritual creatures, extraterrestrial creatures and so on, humanoid and otherwise, with many names and many forms. We respected them or we went to war with them. Either way, one thing is certain, they were evident and without question.

It is theorized that these beings still exist, carrying on in our rivers, lakes and oceans, our forests and our fields, our basements and attics, under the earth and beyond the borders of our realm. However, due to the creation and growth of Christianity, as well as the development of industry and technology, we shifted our focus and rearranged our priorities. As a result, coexistence with the aforementioned began to die. We fought them off or ignored them, and with mankind's transformation, they no longer wanted to coexist with us.

Now, so much time has passed that we've lost the knowledge, aside from what we read in books or hear from our fathers and our father's fathers. Even so, I'm sure that the details have been diluted throughout the centuries. It's certainly dispiriting to say the least.

The Satanic Order av Wyrd respects and aspires to bond, congregate, collaborate, and if nothing else, uphold the traditions and legends of those great beings that held such power in our realm, once upon a time. Many of the Fae overlap the Vaesen in that they're a common creature within both cultures. Nevertheless, we honor them with our acknowledgement. The following is a list of the Vaesen and the Fae. Behold:

The Vaesen

- Älvor: Älvor is the folkloric collective for Nature Spirits who, at dusk and dawn, can be seen dancing over meadows, fields, and mossy patches. They are Elves, and their female counterparts Faeries. It is common for the Faeries to be heard, often as birds chirping. Where the Elves dance, a ring of either unnaturally healthy or unnaturally sparsely growing grass appears. Sometimes the ring consists of fungi and it is in fact a ring-growing fungus that fertilizes the grass and gives rise to this phenomenon. Fulfilling their needs in a river dance inevitably leads to illness and misfortune.

  The Elves' main role is as a pathogen. A person who has "got the faeries" is often thought to have had diseases inflicted on them, by them, and, when equal cures are equally assumed, a strong counterblowing, for example, with a bellows, has a curative effect. They come in many forms, depending on their mood, time of year, environment, and who is watching. They can appear as a mist or frogs or insects, and, sometimes, they're completely invisible.They live in communities in hills, in meadows or bogs, and are ruled over by a faery queen or a faery king, or both.

  Never find yourself on their bad side. They're very unpredictable. Protect your infants from the Älvor by placing steel in their cradles. Protect yourselves by concealing on yourselves the same.

- Askafroa: The Askafroa or the wives of the Ash tree, are malevolent female creatures that live in the Ash tree. They can be highly dangerous if you aren't careful. Once upon a time, the respect for them was so great that one dared not go near a mature Ash tree after dark.

The Satanic Order av Wyrd still respects their boundaries and takes necessary precautions as not to disrespect or anger the Askafroa. She is the soul of the Ash tree and her life is bound with its existence. If you are near an Ash tree on Ash Wednesday, before sunrise, pour water on the roots of the tree and recite these words: "I now carry out this rite so that you will cause us no harm."

- **Gruvrå:** The Gruvrå rules over places with mining deposits. She acts like a witch, an animal, a gray-bearded old man or a bat and often scares away people who want to use the ore. She can also appear as an elegant lady, tall and handsome, often elegantly dressed in a light gray dress.

  If she's in a really good mood, she could show you where suitable oatmeal is or warn of accidents. She punishes all who do not show her and her mountain the proper respect. She is not interested in luring men. She prefers solitude and silence within the eternal darkness at the heart of the mountain.

- **Nisse:** One of the most popular Vaesen, the Nisse watches over the farmstead and all the animals and people that live there. If you have a Nisse on your property, you will have prosperity and will be made aware of any impending danger. He's ill mannered and bad tempered, and he prefers to be left alone.

  The Nisse can take the shape of a black cat or a large toad. So be aware and try to avoid treating either of these types of creatures poorly, if you happen upon them on your property. Just don't treat them too well. They may avoid their duties to consume the fruits of your kindness.

- **Havsfru:** The Havsfru or Mermaid/Merman is a powerful being and rules over the waves, wind, and all sea creatures. If you happen upon one, you'll do well to make an offering, coin, food, clothing, and so on. In return, you'll be safe from any seafaring related dangers and your fishing bounties will be great.

She or he can appear as many creatures of the sea, seals, dolphins, and the most commonly recalled, a beautiful woman or handsome man with gills and a fish tail in place of his or her legs.

- **Jättar:** The Jättar or Giant is an enormous, primordial creature that has lived in our realm long before us. They are insanely strong and extremely clumsy, as well as dimwitted. Keep your distance from a Giant with a taste for human flesh.

  But there are agreeable Giants, as well. The implications of having a Giant on your side are great and powerful. A more loyal companion there is not.

- **Kvarngubbe:** The Kvarngubbe is a spirit being or Gnome who lives in mills and either helps the miller or opposes him. He is strong and a skilled violinist.
- **Skogsrå:** The Skogsrå is the mistress of the forest, a nymph that appears as a small, beautiful woman from the front and has a hollow back and tail when seen from behind. She appears to convey a seemingly friendly temperament. But do not cross her.

  Those who are enticed into following her into the forest are never seen again. It is said that any human man who has intercourse with the Skogsrå becomes an introvert, as his soul has remained with her. If the seduced man is a hunter, he may be rewarded with good luck in the hunt, but should he be unfaithful to the Skogsrå, he will be punished with numerous accidents.

- **Källrå:** The Källrå is the guardian of the spring. Most often remaining invisible or taking the form of a frog, they protect the water source from those who would show ill will or use the spring without leaving a gift.

- **Skeppsrå:** The Skeppsrå is more or less the same as the Kvarngubbe. However, instead of a mill, the Skeppsrå resides on shiPsalm He too will either help or oppose you. Be respectful.
- **Sjörå:** The Sjörå is the powerful sprite of the mountain pool or lake. She is a seductive creature, often featured sitting and combing her long, sweeping, dark green hair with delight. Unlike the mermaid, she walks on two legs. Expect to leave an offering of tobacco or coin if you want to live. Be respectful or become fish food.
- **Näcken:** Näcken are male water spirits who play enchanted songs on the violin, luring women and children to drown in lakes or streams. However, not all of these spirits are necessarily malevolent.

  Näcken can be sensed by the presence of flowering water lilies. If you see these, place a knife in the shore before fishing or going for a swim. If you see Näcken, he'll be recognized by his long dark green hair, black eyes, and green slimy skin. But his appearance varies with some out-of-place characteristics, such as horses hooves, a third eye, frog eyes, horns, webbed fingers and toes.

- **Bäckahäst:** The Bäckahäst is a majestic white horse that can appear near rivers, particularly during foggy weather. Anyone who climbs onto its back will not be able to get off again. The horse is known to then jump into the river, drowning the rider. The Bäckahäst can also be harnessed and made to plough, either by trying and failing to trick a person or because the person has tricked the horse into doing this work by use of a steel bit.

  The Bäckahäst can also appear gray and black, or even shades of blue. It has pointed, razor-sharp teeth. It's in many aspects like Näcken and some people believe that it is Näcken in disguise.

- **Troll:** The Troll is a secretive creature that lives with many others in mountains and hills, far from humans. They are much like us, in that they get married and have children, they brew beer, bake bread, mine gems and ore, and commune in civil manners with the other Trolls. However, they can live much longer than us.

They've been known to steal whatever they can. If you live close to Trolls, take the necessary precautions. They may even steal a newly born child (replacing the newborn with a Changeling), a mother, or adolescent boys and girls.

It is a common misconception that Trolls are gigantic, grotesque creatures. Some of them are. But some of them can be difficult to tell apart from a human. The female Troll, for example, can be even more alluring and beautiful than a human female.

- **Vittror:** The Vittror live underground, are invisible most of the time, and have their own cattle (which are also invisible). When they are visible, however, they look like you or me, just much smaller. They wear clothing similar to our own and they have their own goats and cattle.

  Most of the time, Vittror are rather distant and do not meddle in human affairs, but are fearsome when enraged. They can make your life very miserable or even dangerous. They do whatever it takes to drive you away, even arrange accidents that will harm or even kill you. Even now, people have rebuilt or moved houses in order not to block a Vittror-Way or moved from houses that are deemed a Vittror-Place (vittrorställe) because of bad luck, although this is rather uncommon.

- **Vättar:** The Vättar is not much bigger than a rat and can appear with the characteristics of rats, toads, mice, hedgehogs, etc. They enjoy being close to people and are drawn to farms and villages. They live underground. Their dwellings lie close to a farmstead, often under a large tree or barn, and sometimes even under the farmhouse itself.
- **Mara:** Mara is a mare, a night hag, who appears as a hideous female creature and torments people and animals at night. She can crawl onto the chest of sleeping people and squeeze the air and the very life out of them. The sleeper will wake in a cold sweat with the

sensation of being suffocated. You may have seen her during a bout with sleep paralysis.

No one is truly safe from Mara. But you can slow her down by piling hair or shoes or things of that nature near a window or door. She'll be compelled to count every stand or shoe and the like until the deed is done, leaving no time to harm anyone or thing.

- **Varulv:** The Varulv, werewolf, is a tragic creature, doomed to live his life with the fear of harming his loved ones when the change comes over him. But, in the cases where the transformation happens at will, the Varulv is a bloodthirsty creature. The change can happen in many ways, crawling through the amniotic sac of a foal, being bitten by another, curses, skinwalking, and so on. He appears as a humanoid wolf.
- **Lyktgubbe:** The Lyktgubbe is a Will-o'-the-wisp, an atmospheric ghostly light seen by travelers at night, especially over bogs, swamps or marshes. This light can change shape and color, and it moves erratically and quickly. But it really isn't the light that moves itself, so much as it is the old lantern man.

  The old lantern man is thought to be a troubled soul of a dead person who once cheated during a property dispute. He can be malicious and lead people astray or to their doom. But he may also help you, when you're lost, to find your way home or desired destination.

- **Draugr:** The Draugr is the spirit of a wicked person, full of hate for the living, that continues to spread fear wherever it goes, even after its death. It appears as a horrific monstrous creature, pitch black, often with claws and jagged teeth. They will suck the life out of you and may even devour you. They cannot be in the sun, or they will be petrified.
- **Nattramn:** The Nattramn or night raven is a restless soul of a criminal or unbaptized child that is doomed to spend its afterlife in the form of a raven. It can be seen at night, swooping over the

ground, followed by a bloodcurdling scream or an odd creaking noise. It always flies low and is a cruel, aggressive being, using its talons and beak to seriously hurt the living.

- **Kraken:** The Kraken is a fearsome sea monster with numerous fins and tentacles that lurks below the waves of the North Sea. It usually sleeps in darkness, at the depths of the sea, and rarely surfaces. On the surface, it is commonly mistaken for an island and is said, by some, to extend 130 miles. It can devour entire ships and is inclined to do so, because it has the taste for human blood.
- **Gloson:** The Gloson is an aggressive, enormous pig. Its jaws are filled with huge tusks and its eyes glow a fire red. When it grunts, the ground trembles.
- **Drake:** The Drake or dragon is the most dangerous and notorious creature. They are monsters with coiling, snakelike bodies, huge leathery wings, and razor-sharp claws and teeth. They're smart, malicious, and greedy, and they can spit fire.
- **Sjöodjur:** The Sjöodjur or sea serpent is a gigantic, malicious, hungry creature that lives in caves and crevices around the coastline. They lie in wait for shoals of fish and very rarely come up to the surface. They can use their gaze to hypnotize humans and cattle into walking right into their mouths, and they can capsize ships to devour the crew.
- **Lindorm:** The Lindorm is a gigantic and horrifying snake, the king of the serpents. It appears with a white mane that grows on its neck and has long, fearsome fangs, and can spray corrosive venom from its mouth. If one can kill and eat its flesh, he or she can gain magical powers, such as the ability to see the future, heal, talk to animals, etc.

The Lindorm likes to live under old oak trees. There, it guards its treasures. But, if you manage to see one out and about, you may recognize it by its ability to bite its own tail and roll around like a wheel.

***

If you wish to learn more about the Vaesen, Google has many sources. However, it can get rather problematic finding complete lists and direct feedback on each. If you have the money and the time, it would be well worth it to go to Grimfrost's website and purchase a copy of Johan Egerkrans' book, Vaesen: Spirits and Monsters of Scandinavian Folklore.

The Fae

- **Brownie:** Brownies are known as helpers for farmers. They tend to do outdoor tasks during the night such as shoveling hay, feeding the sheep, etc. They are approximately three feet tall and have pointed ears, brown complexions, and brown working clothes.

  Brownies are drawn towards the most deserving of families. People who work the hardest and who most need extra help usually fall into this category. When Brownies stick with a family for an elongated period of time and are generally respected and treated well, they will bring good luck to the household. They tend to be predominantly nocturnal, shy, and will do your household chores if you mind your own business.

- **Pixie:** When you think of the different types of Faeries, the image that emerges in thought, especially if you're not familiar with the Fae, is probably the Pixie. Pixies are only about four inches tall and tend to live in the gardens and woods. They are humanlike figures and delicate wings that move extremely fast, like a hummingbird's.

  Even though Pixies tend to enjoy contact with humans, they're very cunning and mischievous and can delight in leading humans astray. They don't understand human desperation or pain. So, while they play a lot of jokes for fun, these jokes may not seem funny to people and can cause serious harm to the human. However, as long as you respect them, they'll usually respect you as well.

- **Banshee:** The Banshee is a female-spirit type of faery that predicts death. Her Cry of Death is typically an omen. She can appear in many different forms, but she is known to appear as a beautiful, young woman, a stately matron, or an old, ugly hag. Although, she is rarely seen, but certainly heard. If you hear the Banshee cry, you or someone near you is going to die.

- **Goblin:** The term Goblin can be meant as a generalization for all Fae who are mischievous and/or malevolent. However, the Goblin itself is also a specific multifaceted race of Fae. They come in many forms, colors, sizes, and so on. But they're commonly seen as roughly two feet tall, with long, pointy, or flat noses, batlike ears, with a dull gray or green hue.

  They're known as the thieves and villains of the Fae realm. They are everywhere and, if their attention is drawn to you, you've no hope. However, if they decide that they admire you, you'll live favorably until death.

- **Leprechaun:** Leprechauns appear as super small, aged men dressed in green or red. They often wear a pointed cap and love to smoke pipes. They're mainly found in Ireland.

  Most types of Fae don't have set jobs like humans do. Leprechauns are the exception. They are, first and foremost, cobblers, but can also act as bankers in the fairy world. Legend says that Leprechauns are constantly crafting shoes because other types of Faeries wear out their shoes nightly during their seemingly endless dances or balls.

  If you happen upon a Leprechaun, treat him with the utmost respect and you may be handsomely rewarded with wealth and/or music lessons, as Leprechauns are fond of music, especially the fiddle, harp, and the bodhrán. But be careful: they are very tricky and mischievous.

- **Elf:** Out of all the Faeries, Elves are closest to humans in size and stature. Elves have high cheekbones and angular features. They are also said to have mesmerizing eyes and pointed ears.

  People in many cultures still believe in the Elves. In fact, many of the caves in Iceland are protected by the government because three-quarters of the residents believe that Elves reside in the area. Elves are the types of Faeries that protect and maintain the forest. They are usually tied to the specific forest that they protect and live in groups.

  They are very strong, fast, agile, intelligent, and wise. Do not cross an Elf. You will surely die.

- **Changeling:** The Changeling is not quite Fae and not quite human. They're in a league of their own but also part of both worlds simultaneously. A Changeling is a Fae child that has been swapped for a human child.

  The changeling will grow up with human parents, but will not appear as a normal human child. They may appear sickly and won't grow in size like a normal child, and may have notable physical characteristics, such as an unusual beard or abnormally long teeth, or they might appear to be unusually healthy, as a bodybuilder, without the need to bodybuild. They may also display intelligence far beyond their apparent years, as well as possess uncanny insight. A common way that a changeling could identify itself is through displaying unusual behavior when it thinks it is alone, such as jumping about, dancing or playing multiple instruments, even talking to others, who aren't actually visibly there, in full conversation. They can have superhuman strength or can be tremendously weak, depending on the reason for the switch.

  If you have the means and talent, you will know a Changeling when you see it. Respect him or her and reveal your knowledge of their being a Changeling. You will be noticeably rewarded shortly thereafter, in one form or another.

- **Dryad:** The Dryad is a tree Faery. Much like the Askafroa, if the tree dies, so does the Dryad. You will know that you've come upon a Dryad tree when the tree is very old and looks like it has an emerging face in the trunk, but naturally formed. As you approach the tree, you'll feel an ecstatic, calming, joyful sensation in much the same way as the Schumann waves interact with us.

  Dryads are the most gentle type of Fae. They are very empathetic, sympathetic, and pure. If you haven't much experience communicating or dealing with the Fae, the Dryad is most suitable for beginners.

- **Gnomes:** The Gnome is a multifaceted name, in that there are many different types. The most common is a type of Fae that lives among tree roots in various forests around the world, the Forest Gnome. They can be a max of a foot in height, but are nearly seven times stronger than humans. They are extremely fast and their sense of sight is heightened to that of a hawk.

  They are known to be very selfless, when it comes to wounded animals. As a result, every forest animal is more than willing to help the Gnome when needed. So beware, if you happen to offend a Gnome.

- Furthermore, Gnomes have an affinity for precious gems and stones. They're the best gem cutters and jewelers in existence. As a result, they have immense collections within their dwellings.

- **Kelpie:** The Kelpie is a shape-changing aquatic spirit. Kelpies are said to haunt rivers and streams, usually in the shape of a horse. These are malevolent spirits.

  The Kelpie may appear as a tame pony beside a river. It is particularly attractive to children, but they should take care, for once on its back, its sticky magical hide will not allow them to dismount. Once trapped in this way, the Kelpie will drag the child into the river and then eat him.

  They may also materialize as a beautiful young woman, hoping to lure young men to their death. Alternatively, they might take on the form of a hairy human lurking by the river, ready to jump out at unsuspecting travelers and crush them to death in a vice-like grip. Whatever the form, you'll rarely escape a Kelpie that has it out for you.

Furthermore, despite form, they can call forth floods or sink-holes or tidal waves to drown you before you even catch a glimpse of them. This is the wrath of the Kelpie. Be warned.

Fortunately, the Kelpie isn't always so deadly. They may warn you of an impending storm, save you from drowning, help you in your fishing endeavors, etc. As always, if you encounter a Kelpie and aren't already dead, treat them with respect and make an offering.

- **Salamanders:** Salamanders are fire spirits. Without them, fire cannot exist. Their assistance is required for creating even the smallest bit of flame, even that on a match.

  Their help can be invited, but they can be mischievous. A pro-voked Salamander may cause fires to burn out of control, especially since they don't fully comprehend the results of their actions. So take precaution.

  Typically they appear as lizards, though they are sometimes viewed in a more typical Faery fashion. They've even been known to appear as small balls of light. Salamanders are reported to possess the ability to change their size at will, either extending or diminishing as they please.

- **Selkie:** A Selkie is a type of fae that has the ability to change from a seal into a human being at will by shedding its skin. They've been known to congregate with humans. It is said that, if you take the shed skin of a Selkie after they've become a human, they will be yours. But she will spend her time longing for the sea, her true home, and will often be seen gazing longingly at the ocean. She may even bear several children by her human husband, but once she discovers her skin, she will immediately return to the sea and abandon the children she loved.

- **Boggart:** Always malevolent, the household Boggart is said to be a Brownie turned bad. The Boggart will follow its family wherever they flee. It is said that the boggart crawls into people's beds at night and puts a clammy hand on their faces. Sometimes he strips the bedsheets off them. Sometimes a boggart will also pull on a person's ears. They're known to sabotage household items or parts of the house or its structure, stairs, doors, windows, plumbing and electrical, and so on.
- **Mermaids, Dragons, Will-o'-the-Wisps, and the Like:** These Fae are the same as the Vaesen descriptions made previously.

Let it be known that the line between fantasy and reality is blurry and reality is commonly known as being stranger than fiction. With so many creatures becoming extinct, including entire human civilizations, and so many more living beings in numerous categories being discovered or resurfacing regularly, how can anyone claim to know what is or isn't out there? If nothing else, paying your respects and upholding tradition is a fine discipline. But, if you can incorporate this discipline into a fervent belief and that fusion yields substantial, positive, hard results, then you will be fortuitous, and powerful, and part of something of which very few people have the knowledge and privilege.

CHAPTER IX

Additional Figures Honored by SOW: The Figures av Glory

There are many other figures that maintained a powerful prominence, once upon a time, that the Satanic Order av Wyrd still honors today. These figures may not necessarily be thought of as existing in our realm of reality. However, we like to entertain the idea that they may actually exist and, if they do (and even if they don't), we honor and respect them for their indisputable greatness and power, as well as what they represent. The following is a list of those figures and their descriptions, as well as what they represent or symbolize. Behold!

- **The Imp King:** The legend of the Imp King dates back to the twelfth century and expounds an account of how a Satan stole a child and placed an Imp in the cradle. The Imp grew up with a hateful grudge against said Satan and eventually returned to Hell where he started a revolution. He called upon all of the other Imps and Hellhounds and all other alleged minor beasts to join his fight for revenge.

  He led the largest army of so-called lesser demons into the throne room of Hell where he was ultimately victorious. Upon his victory, he grew a crown of horns and was deemed the Imp King. The opposing higher ranking demons surrendered and volunteered to be his slaves forever.

This story is said to be a false timeworn tale and its pages were either removed from the internet completely or archived and are very difficult to recover. Regardless, it is our assessment that the creation of the story itself means it has substantiality and can easily be regarded as a timeless tale for centuries to come. *With our help, it will be.*

We honor the Imp King and his story because of what they symbolize: rebellion, strength and determination, revenge, success, and power, and from a generally regarded evil perspective, no less.. The Imp King is the perfect motivational tool for the Lokessen. All, Hail Victory! All, Hail the Imp King! All, Hail the Satan, Loke!

- סָמָאֵל (**Samael**): Samael is known by many names and for many positions. He is the Venom of God, a fallen archangel, Death, a master seducer and the chief destroyer, a Satan, the Serpent or Serpent's Accomplice of Eden, partner of Lilith, father of Cain, archenemy of Israel, and the father of the Sword of Asmodai. However, it is commonly understood that he remains loyal to God. Regardless, he condones the sins of man and regularly accomplishes malevolent, sexual, and violent deeds. For these, the Satanic Order av Wyrd pays homage to Samael. All, Hail Death, Destruction, and Sexual Deviance! All, Hail Samael. All, Hail the Satan, Loke!
- לִילִית (**Lilith**): Lilith is the Queen of Demons and was the first wife of Adam of Eden. However, it is said that she rebelled against both Adam and God. It is said that she fled into the dark forest and perpetually mated with Asmodeus, the Prince of Demons. Together, they introduced many of what are known to be Vaesen and Fae as well as numerous types of demonic figures and poisonous, vile animals.

She loves intercourse and hates human babies. In fact, she's been known to murder human babies and sexually assault human men while they sleep, a Succubus of sorts. So sleep with one eye open.

She is also thought to have procreated with Samael. It is said that she became a serpent and Samael rode upon her back into the Garden of Eden, where they tempted Eve into partaking of the

Forbidden Fruit, fruit that grew from a tree in which she'd created early on with these malicious intentions. It is said that God knew this and forbade Adam from eating it.

Lilith is a common figure in many Black Magick organizations and in sub-Satanic cultures. She is often worshipped and serves as a symbol for femininity, as well as freedom, rebellion, evil, Black Magick, revenge, sexual indiscrimination, the revealing of truths, etc. The Satanic Order av Wyrd pays homage to Lilith for her tale and what she symbolizes. All, Hail Freedom, Black Magick, Evil, and Truth! All, Hail Lilith! All, Hail the Satan, Loke!

- **The Baba Yaga:** The Baba Yaga appears as a horrifying, ferocious, deformed old woman, known to reside in a cabin or hut that lay on two giant, traveling chicken legs. She's a witch or sorceress. But her humanity is debatable. She may very well be something else entirely.

  She's been known to eat children regularly. She's also been known to be quite sexually malicious, forcing men to pleasure her in exchange for their deaths. You do not want to upset the Baba Yaga.

  Regardless of her wrathful, evil behavior, she is well known for her severe ambiguity and misleadership. As a result, you may be awarded kindness from the Baba Yaga if she so chooses. This means great wealth, power, or general success in your endeavors.

  We pay homage to the Baba Yaga. May she continue to govern for all eternity. All, Hail Cannibalism and Sexual Domination! All, Hail the Baba Yaga! All, Hail the Satan, Loke!

- Διόνυσος **(Dionysus):** Dionysus is the god of the grape-harvest, winemaking and wine (he's also known as the Drunken God), fertility, orchards and fruit, vegetation, insanity, ritual madness, religious ecstasy, festivity and theatre. His wine, music, and ecstatic dance free his followers from self-conscious fear and Amy other inhibitions, and subvert the oppressive restraints of the powerful. Those who partake of his mysteries are believed to become possessed and empowered by the god himself.

He is known by many names and, in some tales, is of unknown origins. However, many claim he is a product of Zeus and Persephone and is thought to be the chthonic, underworld aspect of Zeus. Strangely enough, he was also thought to have died and rebirthed under an additional mother.

In many ways, his characteristics mirror Loke's. We in SOW like to think that if they happened upon one another, they would get along exquisitely, perhaps even create a child together, a child that would mean a record-breaking certain destruction and debauchery across the multiverse. Regardless of hypotheticals and wishful thinking, we pay homage to Dionysus! All, Hail Sex, Drugs, and Rock & Roll! All, Hail Dionysus! All, Hail the Satan, Loke!

- **Lyssa:** Following suit, in light of Dionysus, we also honor Lyssa. Lyssa is the goddess of mad rage and frenzy, as well as rabies in animals. She is said to be the daughter of the primordial deity, Nyx (night), that emerged from the blood of the Titan, Uranus, after he was castrated by his son, Cronus. She can drive people and animals mad, causing them to hallucinate and become extremely violent and murderous.

  The Satanic Order av Wyrd feels that madness is the raw nature of man and a doorway to secret realms as well as the answers to a myriad of mysteries in the universe. Additionally, anyone who is born directly from the blood of a vicious act and carries with them blind rage and madness has a place in our hearts. We pay homage to Lyssa! All, Hail Blind Rage and Madness! All, Hail Lyssa! All, Hail the Satan, Loke!

- **Angra Mainyu, Ahriman:** Ahriman, or Angra Mainyu (meaning "destructive spirit"), is the originator of death and all that is evil in the world. He cocreating the Earth with Ahura Mazda, the righteous, supreme god. Together, they were born of the universe and automatically chose their own paths.

Angra Mainyu's essential nature is expressed in his primary title—Druj, "the Lie," in the assembly of greed, wrath, and envy. To aid him in attacking the light, Ahura Mazda, Angra Mainyu created a horde of demons embodying envy and similar qualities, known as Daevas. Despite the chaos and suffering affected in the world by his onslaught, believers expect Angra Mainyu to be defeated in the end of time by Ahura Mazda. Confined to their own realm, his demons will devour each other, and his own existence will be quenched.

We pay homage to Angra Mainyu and his Daevas. All Hail Death and All that is Evil! All Hail Angra Mainyu and his Daevas! All Hail the Satan, Loke!

- **Pan:** Pan is the god of the wild, shepherds and flocks, nature of mountain wilds, rustic music and impromptus, and companion of the nymphs. He has the hindquarters, legs, and horns of a goat, in the same manner as a faun or satyr. With his homeland in rustic Arcadia, he is also recognized as the god of fields, groves, wooded glens and often affiliated with sex; because of this, Pan is connected to fertility and the season of Spring.

  He is of unknown origins, but some believe that his parents are Hermes and Penelope. Others say that his mother, Penelope, slept with 108 suitors, and Pan is the end result. Regardless, no one truly knows from where Pan came.

  It is said that Pan can produce a scream that is so frightening that anyone and anything who hears it will flee in fear. This is where the word *panic* originates. The Pan flute is also a reference to Pan and/or the one who would have been his mate: Syrinx, a beautiful wood nymph, flees from Pan's attention and her fellow goddesses turn her into a river reed in order to hide her from him. As the winds blow through the reeds, they make a gentle musical sound. Because he does not know which reed Syrinx is, he cuts several reeds from the group and sets them in a line to make the musical instrument, the Syrinx or Pan flute, in memory of his lost love.

Mythical stories of Pan's have flourished and he continues to be a figure representing the ancient mystery of the forest, the hunt, and wildlife. Like many Gods of Ancient Greece, Pan embodies many of the qualities of the world over which he ruled. He is depicted as energetic, sometimes frightening, with the wild, unbridled creative force of nature that makes him an interesting, and often entertaining, character. However, once upon a time, he was shunned by most and often resorted to trickery and malevolence in order to seduce a mate or claim an ally.

Pan, with his whimsical, wild, music loving demeanor, and also his panic inducing, frightful nature, and his debaucherous sexuality make him one to which the Satanic Order av Wyrd pays homage. He is in many ways akin to our Satan, Loke. All, Hail Debauchery, Wild Nature, Frightful Spirit, and the Hunt! All, Hail Pan! All, Hail the Satan, Loke!

- **Der Erlkönig (The Elf King or The Goblin King):** The Goblin King was first noticed in a poem written in 1782 by a man by the name of Johann Wolfgang Von Goethe. The poem tells the story of a boy riding home on horseback in his father's arms. He is frightened when he is courted by the Erlkönig, a powerful, terrifying, and strangely inviting, supernatural being. The boy's father, however, cannot see or hear the creature and tells the boy that his imagination is playing tricks on him. The boy grows increasingly terrified by what he hears from the Erlkönig, but his father tells him that the things he thinks he sees and hears are only the sights and sounds of nature on that dark and stormy night. When the Erlkönig eventually seizes the boy, the father spurs on his horse, but when he arrives home his son is dead.

The original poem is as follows:

Who rides there so late through the night dark and drear?
The father it is, with his infant so dear;
He holdeth the boy tightly clasp'd in his arm,

He holdeth him safely, he keepeth him warm.

"My son, wherefore seek'st thou thy face thus to hide?"
"Look, father, the Erlkönig is close by our side!
Dost see not the Erlkönig, with crown and with train?"
"My son, 'tis the mist rising over the plain."

"Oh, come, thou dear infant! oh come thou with me!
Full many a game I will play there with thee;
On my strand, lovely flowers their blossoms unfold,
My mother shall grace thee with garments of gold."

"My father, my father, and dost thou not hear
The words that the Erlkönig now breathes in mine ear?"
"Be calm, dearest child, 'tis thy fancy deceives;
'Tis the sad wind that sighs through the withering leaves."

"Wilt go, then, dear infant, wilt go with me there?
My daughters shall tend thee with sisterly care
My daughters by night their glad festival keep,
They'll dance thee, and rock thee, and sing thee to sleep."

"My father, my father, and dost thou not see,
How the Erlkönig his daughters has brought here for me?"
"My darling, my darling, I see it aright,
'Tis the aged gray willows deceiving thy sight."

"I love thee, I'm charm'd by thy beauty, dear boy!
And if thou'rt unwilling, then force I'll employ."
"My father, my father, he seizes me fast,
Full sorely the Erlkönig has hurt me at last."

The father now gallops, with terror half wild,
He grasps in his arms the poor shuddering child;

He reaches his courtyard with toil and with dread,—
The child in his arms finds he motionless, dead.

We're well aware that an Elf is, in most cases, a male Faery.
We're also aware that a Goblin is a twisted, malevolent, malicious
Elf, and other Fae with similar qualities, as well as their own entity
entirely. It is also common for the Fae, especially the Faeries and
Goblins, to participate in the act of Changelingery.

However, in the human realm of existence, we tend to focus
more on things that immediately affect us, as opposed to what is
happening with our missing children on the other side, on the Fae
side, and we certainly don't seem to care about the Fae and their
motives. Furthermore, even those who care to afford the Fae time
and strive for knowledge as to why they do what they do, they
usually don't know any more than what they did in the beginning.

We do know, however, that they like to take children and they'll
even take adults, at times. It's been said that, when adults are taken,
they initially feel as though they are in a paradise, a perpetual
party or ball, and they dance. Unfortunately, if the adult is taken
for punishment or if the Fae mean ill will, the adult won't be able
to stop dancing, until death; and, even then, they're soul may be
trapped in the Fae realm for eternity.

The Fae may not always reach the cradle in time, when intending
to take an infant, and, being that they still desire the child, rectify
their tardiness by taking the child in the not so distant future. In
these cases, replacing the human child with one of their own would
be a futile and fruitless effort. When a child is taken, it is usually
because the Fae sees the child as an object of beauty to be collected
and detained and/or enslaved, or the child is viewed as something
more that will be raised as their own.

Using this logic, the Satanic Order av Wyrd hereby dubs the
Erlkönig, Goblin King. When you hear the name, Goblin King,
you may think of David Bowie's character in The Labyrinth. Well,
in this context, he's not at all far off from der Erlkönig.

The Satanic Order av Wyrd pays homage to the Goblin King, for his malicious, malevolent, powerful, terrifying, and creepily inviting characteristics. It's everything we look for in an effective villain and many of the characteristics we look for in the ideal Lokessen. All, Hail Malevolence, Power, Terror, Strangely Alluring qualities, and Thievery. All, Hail the Goblin King. All, Hail the Satan, Loke!

- **Efnysien:** Efnysien is the sadistic anti-hero in Welsh mythology, appearing mainly in the tale of Branwen ferch Llŷr, the second branch of the Mabinogi. He is the catalyst of the tale's ultimate tragedy, and is largely responsible for the destruction of both Ireland and the Island of the Mighty. He is described variously by modern scholars as warped, perverted, malicious, and psychopathic. He brings with him rage, accompanied by a "horrific orgy of violence. … His actions are deliberately staged to inflict the most profound damage to the weak points of the social fabric around him."

  Efnysien is often considered to be one of the most vivid and interesting characters to appear in the four branches, concerning the oldest prose in the literature of Britain, the Mabinogi. Among those who are aware of the four branches, Efnysien has commonly been compared to other trickster figures, such as the Irish hero, Bricriu Nemtheanga, and the Norse god, our Satan, Loke. In some circles, it is said that Efnysien and Loke are one and the same. It's easy to entertain this notion, being that Loke was all over the multiverse at one point in time in many forms.

  The Satanic Order av Wyrd pays homage to Efnysien for nearly all the same reasons as we do our beloved Satan, Loke. All, Hail Perversion, Maliciousness, Psychopathy, Destruction, and Hate! All, Hail Efnysien! All, Hail the Satan, Loke!

***

These figures of theology, folklore, and myth are materialized in literature and, for some, physical entities somewhere within our realm or within the multiverse. To others, being materialized in literature is a creation or birth that makes them just as palpable as their own existence. In this sense, reality is nothing more than perception and perception is a delusion based on nothing more than an illusion. In context, I'm no more real than the Goblin King, the Imp King, or Bugs Bunny. I may be even less real, in this form of thinking. Afterall, I don't have books written about me or shows based on my antics that immortalize my efforts and deeds or misdeeds, etc.

The application of philosophy set aside, the Satanic Order av Wyrd honors these figures for their symbolism and their powerful, influential example, for their greatness. All, Hail the Figures av Glory! All, Hail the Satan, Loke!

CHAPTER X

The Satanic Order av Wyrd—
Imperative and Requisite Reading

Reading allows one to understand the Earth, its inhabitants, and the universe through the experiences of others. Essentially, by reading, we are tapping into the memories, the factories, or the laboratories of mankind; and, as a result of our ability to quickly access this collective knowledge, reading is without a doubt one of the most fundamental tools for evolutionary prosperity. In the significant words of Plato, "Books give a soul to the universe, wings to the mind, flight to the imagination, and life to everything."

The following list was compiled by me, the Grandmaster, Imp K. Lokessen. I've spent my entire life reading these books, multiple times, in fact, and they've shaped my life into what it is today. Now, obviously, solely reading is no true replacement for hands-on experience and I've had my share of that, as well. Realistically, an amalgam of reading, physical and emotional experience, imagination, talent, and deductive/inductive reasoning is the true approach to knowledge and, by proxy, evolutionary prosperity.

If you truly wish to be an Adept Lokessen of the Satanic Order av Wyrd, the following list is your arsenal for success. Handle with care and study diligently. Heed this suggestion, for, when the time comes for you to stand before us to prove your competency and your significance to our cause, you will be tested and cross-examined, in a myriad of ways, and a large portion of this process will concern your aptitude, retention, and practical application.

Narratives and Nonfiction

- Anton Szandor LaVey: *The Satanic Bible*
- Anton Szandor LaVey: *The Devil's Notebook*
- Anton Szandor LaVey: *Satan Speaks!*
- Anton Long: *The Sinister Way: Order of Nine Angles*
- Carl Jung: *Man and His Symbols*
- Ben Hecht: *Guide for the Bedevilled*
- Ben Hecht: *The Kingdom of Evil* (a continuation of *Fantazius Mallare*)
- Robert Eisler: *Man Into Wolf; An Anthropological Interpretation of Sadism, Masochism, and Lycanthropy*
- Peter Viereck: *Metapolitics: The Roots of the Nazi Mind*
- Wilhelm Reich: *The Function of the Orgasm*
- Friedrich Nietzsche: *Beyond Good and Evil*
- Friedrich Nietzshe: *The Antichrist*
- Benjamin Walker: *The Esoteric Encyclopedia of Man*
- Daniel Mannix: *History of Torture*
- Daniel Mannix: *The Hell-fire Club*
- Sigmund Freud: *The Interpretation of Dreams*
- Anatole France: *Revolt of the Angels*
- Peter A. Schock: *Romantic Satanism: Myth and the Historical Moment in Blake, Shelley, and Byron*
- Neil Forsyth: *The Satanic Epic*
- Sterling Boutell, C.B. Boutell: *Speak of the Devil: An Anthology of Demonology*
- Joris K. Huysmans: *La-Bas*
- Asbjorn Dyrendal, James R. Lewis, Jesper AA. Petersen: *The Invention of Satanism*
- Per Faxneld, Jesper AA. Petersen: *The Devil's Party: Satanism in Modernity*
- George Makari: *The Soul Machine*

170

Norse Theology, Cosmology, and Folklore

- Snorri Sturluson: *Poetic Edda*
- Snorri Sturluson: *Prose Edda*
- Tacticus: *Germania*
- Lee M. Hollander: *Old Norse Poems*
- Johan Egerkrans: *Vaesen: Spirits and Monsters of Scandinavian Folklore*
- Johan Egerkrans: *Norse Gods*

Black Magick

- Anton Szandor LaVey: *The Satanic Rituals*
- Anton Long: *NAOS: A Practical Guide to Modern Magick*
- Joseph H. Peterson: *John Dee's Five Books of Mystery: Original Sourcebook of Enochian Magic*
- William R. Sandbach: *The Oera Linda Book, From a Manuscript of the Thirteenth Century*
- John Michael Greer: *The Complete Picatrix: The Occult Classic of Astrological Magic Liber Atratus Edition*
- Unknown Author: *The Grand Grimoire: The Red Dragon*
- Unknown Author: *The Lesser Key of Solomon*
- Aleister Crowley: *Magic in Theory and Practice*
- A. J. Drew: *A Wiccan Bible*
- Bil Linzie: *Drinking at the Well of Mimir*
- Aleister Crowley: *Magic without Tears*
- Charles Godfrey Leland: *Gypsy Sorcery and Fortune Telling*
- H.P. Lovecraft: *Necronomicon*
- Manly P. Hall: *The Secret Teachings of All Ages*
- Rev. St. Synaptyx: *Metaclysmia Discordia*
- Robert Peterson: *Out-of-Body Experiences: How to Have Them and What to Expect*
- Robert Anton Wilson: *Prometheus Rising*

- Thomas Paine: *The Age of Reason*
- Robert Bruce: *Treatise on Astral Projection*
- Aleister Crowley, Hugh Urban: *Unleashing the Beast: Tantra and Sex Magic in Late Victorian England*
- Arthur Edward Waite: *The Book of Ceremonial Magic*
- Brian Froud, Terry Jones: *The Goblin Companion: A Field Guide to Goblins*
- Stephen A. Mitchell: *Witchcraft and Magic in the Nordic Middle Ages*
- Yngona Desmond: *Voluspa: Seidhr As Wyrd Consciousness*

Anarcho-Communism

- Peter Kropotkin: *The Conquest of Bread*
- Peter Kropotkin: *Mutual Aid: A Factor of Evolution*
- Bertrand Russell: *Roads to Freedom*
- James Scott: *Two Cheers for Anarchism: Six Easy Pieces on Autonomy, Dignity, and Meaningful Work and Play*
- Richard D. Wolff: *Democracy at Work: A Cure for Capitalism*
- Noam Chomsky: *Government in the Future*
- Michael Bakunin: *Statism and Anarchy*
- Richard G. Wilkinson, Kate Pickett: *The Spirit Level: Why Greater Equality Makes Societies Stronger*
- Paul Goodman: *Growing Up Absurd: Problems of Youth in the Organized Society*
- David Harvey: *Seventeen Contradictions and the End of Capitalism*
- Steven J. Hirsch, Lucien van der Walt, Dongyoun Hwang, Anthony Gorman: *Anarchism and Syndicalism in the Colonial and Postcolonial World, 1870–1940*
- Nik Brandal, Oivind Bratberg, Dag Einar Thorsen: *The Nordic Model of Social Democracy*
- James Joll: *The Anarchists*
- Vladimir Lenin: *The State and Revolution*
- Daniel Guerin, Noam Chomsky: *Anarchism: From Theory to Practice*

- Errico Malatesta: *The Method of Freedom: An Errico Malatesta Reader*
- William Powell: *The Anarchist Cookbook*
- CrimethInc.: *Recipes for Disaster: An Anarchist Cookbook*

You're welcome, Skål, and Hail the Satan, Loke!

www.ingramcontent.com/pod-product-compliance
Lightning Source LLC
Chambersburg PA
CBHW031433270326
41930CB00007B/688